1973

SHAKESPEARE AND THE VICTORIANS:
Roots of Modern Criticism

UNIVERSITY OF OKLAHOMA PRESS : NORMAN

shakespeare
and the victorians

ROOTS OF MODERN CRITICISM

Aron y. stavisky

Library of Congress Catalog Card Number: 68–31374

Copyright 1969 by the University of Oklahoma Press, Publishing Division of the University. Composed and printed at Norman, Oklahoma, U.S.A., by the University of Oklahoma Press. First edition.

To Nellie
Without whose help this book would not have been written

pReface

No HISTORY of Victorian criticism of Shakespeare has yet been written, doubtless under the assumption that a cultural vacuum exists between Coleridge and the twentieth century. The Victorians are commonly thought to have indulged in gush and adulation when they were not merely repeating Coleridge. This study sets out to chronicle their contribution and assess its relevance to contemporary critical opinion.

The Victorians did not develop their ideas about Shakespeare from within the romantic tradition. Instead, drawing from the eighteenth century, they brought to full flower Malone's historical perspective and the moral criteria of Johnson. Information about Shakespeare was collected and organized on an unprecedented scale, principally through two learned societies: the Shakespeare Society (1840–53), founded by J. P. Collier (1789–1883); and the New Shakspere Society (1873–94), founded by Frederick James Furnivall (1825–1910). Shakespeare was interpreted in terms of this new mass of information much as the natural universe was being first tabulated on the basis of statistics collected by Victorian scientists. Naturally, Shakespeare was subjected to the laws of evolution, his life divided into periods of expansion and contraction, although some critics saw him as a hero who withstood both law and time. Since God was dead, men transferred His attributes to great figures living and dead. Perhaps the most famous twentieth-century work on Shakespeare, Caroline Spurgeon's

Shakespeare's Imagery and What It Tells Us, develops both these Victorian themes. Shakespeare is tabulated in the best nineteenth-century tradition and, at the same time, he heroically transcends the laws that encompass him. Miss Spurgeon's *Five Hundred Years of Chaucer Criticism and Allusion* (*1357–1900*) had been published by Furnivall's Chaucer Society, and the technique of *Shakespeare's Imagery* . . . was anticipated by Furnivall at one of his New Shakspere Society meetings, on October 13, 1876.

The most interesting contribution of Victorian Shakespeare scholarship dealt with an earlier manifestation of what we now call the "two cultures." Furnivall maintained that the verse tests and other statistical tools collected by his New Shakspere Society provided scientific evidence "proving" which parts of the plays attributed to him Shakespeare really wrote. Swinburne, in a long controversy lasting through most of the 1870's, maintained that the essential quality of poetry did not yield itself to scientific analysis. Although Swinburne insisted with all the passion of F. R. Leavis on the poetic value of Shakespeare's art, at the same time he persistently objected to the allegorizing G. Wilson Knight employs today and which we like now to construe as a Victorian vice. Contemporary criticism has assimilated and greatly refined the Victorian historical perspective while discarding its firm ethical emphasis.

The weakness of Victorian Shakespeare criticism was its inability to come to terms with the element of genius in Coleridge, his distinction between Fancy and Imagination, between words applied as decorative art and words fused into something totally new. Victorian critics ignored the metaphor-making function which Coleridge had tried to pin down. Our own investigations of imagery benefit from Freud and his twentieth-century successors who made the wealth of subconscious impulse and association accessible to critics of poetry. Lacking this, the Victorian critics were unable to formulate a theory of imagery.

One reason for so much good modern criticism may be that we have absorbed the historical perspective largely created by the Victorians and coupled with it the romantic imaginative insight, principally as articulated by Coleridge.

ARON Y. STAVISKY

Brooklyn, New York
July 25, 1968

contents

ILLUSTRATIONS

SHAKESPEARE AND THE VICTORIANS
Roots of Modern Criticism

WHOEVER CONSIDERS the revolutions of learning . . . must lament . . . that great part of the labor of every writer is only the destruction of those that went before him. The first care of the builder of a new system is to demolish the fabrics which are standing. The chief desire of him that comments an author is to show how much other commentators have corrupted and obscured him. The opinions prevalent in one age as truths above the reach of controversy are confuted and rejected in another and rise again to reception in remoter times. Thus the human mind is kept in motion without progress.

—Samuel Johnson, Preface to
The Plays of William Shakespeare (1765)

an introduction to victorian criticism

A NUMBER OF CAUSES—not accident—explain why no history of Shakespeare criticism in the Victorian period has yet been written. But the reason for attempting one goes beyond the urge to complete lacunae or the intellectual mountaineering that scales peaks simply because they are there.

Hamlet, in a deceptively simple metaphor, urged his Elsinore players to hold a mirror up to nature, supposing this would show "the very age and body of the time his form and pressure." But whatever playing accomplishes in the alchemy of transmuting words to drama, it is the response to Shakespeare more than to any artist of the past three centuries that illuminates criticism of an age. His work is the mirror in whose reflection we may most conveniently gauge a generation's response, and there seems every reason to believe that the process is continuing. Thus, a generation hence, scholars may conveniently assess the drift of our critical contribution by evaluating the mid-century's response to Shakespeare.

The Victorians brought certain characteristics to the understanding of Shakespeare which were so unlike those of the preceding romantic decades that some particular explanation must be sought. Criticism in the early twentieth century, for example, despite its large claims to originality and emancipation, flowed rather freely from certain Victorian assumptions.

As our own century delights in bringing its first fruits to the altar, applying various forms of analysis to Shakespeare, so the Victorians brought to the art of interpretation two principles of their age: the sense of progressive order, and an intense moral purpose. The earlier twentieth century tended to absorb the Victorian comparative method and to deride the emphasis on ethics, perhaps confounding, like Samuel Butler, all morality with the hypocrite. The Leavis essay which Anne Ridler selects for her *Shakespeare Criticism 1935–1960* proclaims grandly: "We have left Bradley fairly behind";[1] W. W. Lawrence, who dedicated his *Shakespeare's Problem Comedies*[2] to Bradley, chooses for his Victorian butt the now obscure R. G. Moulton, who closely anticipates Bradley and would be more famous but for the appearance of *Shakespearean Tragedy* in 1904. To the reprint of *Shakespeare's Tragic Heroes*, Lily B. Campbell appends two essays deriding Bradley for the intrusion of Victorian morality into the conventions of Elizabethan stagecraft.[3]

Neither the Victorian ethical commitment, so generously criticized, nor the statistical method, generally scanted, is considered characteristic of the romantic achievement directly preceding our

---

[1] London, 1963, p. 133.

[2] New York, 1931. "Critics who look upon Shakespeare's plays as storehouses of moral teaching are naturally severe on Posthumus; we may let R. G. Moulton speak for these" (p. 177). Lawrence tries to invalidate any moral response to *Cymbeline* by citing consecutive Victorian critics who have reached diametrically opposite conclusions. So Moulton is followed by a paragraph beginning: "On the other hand, Posthumus has had his defenders. It is amusing to find that Gervinus praises him for just the quality in which Moulton finds him lacking" (p. 178). Lawrence reconciles ambiguity through recourse to Shakespeare's sources and conventions of morality then extant. The difficulty with rational, classical morality is twofold—first, it ignores the Judeo-Christian literary convention, and second, the absurd is now morally intelligible.

[3] New York, 1960 (1st edition, 1930). Her titles, much in the vein of Leavis, are: "Bradley Revisited: Forty Years After" (p. 241), and "Concerning Bradley's *Shakespearean Tragedy*" (p. 267). These were reprinted from *Studies in Philology*, XLIV, 2 (April, 1947), and *Huntington Library Quarterly*, VII (November, 1949), respectively.

4

period. Indeed, it is significant that Coleridge could sometimes confuse the order of Shakespeare's plays although he wrote Shakespeare criticism principally after Malone's death (1812); Malone, contributing to Steevens' second edition of 1778, had tentatively established the order in which the canon was created.[4] Malone's method was the modern one, comparing records and allusions; we have only to examine E. K. Chambers' ordering in *William Shakespeare: A Study of Facts and Problems* to see how closely Malone's example has been followed.[5] Nicholas Rowe, in the Preface to his edition of 1709, had volunteered that it was utterly impossible to determine the order in which Shakespeare created his canon: "Perhaps we are not to look for his Beginnings, like those of other Authors, among their least perfect Writings; Art had so little, and Nature so large a Share in what he did, that, for ought I know, the Performances of his Youth, as they were the most vigorous, and had the most fire and strength of Imagination in 'em, were the best."[6]

About a century later, Coleridge twice cited *The Tempest* as an early play on intuitive grounds; intuition afforded considerable latitude, and what he said concerning chronology depends on where in Raysor you happen to look.[7] In 1810, he wrote:

Shakespeare's earliest dramas I take to be,
> *Love's Labour's Lost.*
> *All's Well That Ends Well.*
> *Comedy of Errors.*
> *Romeo and Juliet.*

[4] Malone included his essay entitled "An Attempt to Ascertain the Order in Which the Plays of Shakspeare Were Written," prefaced by his "Extracts of Entries on the Books of the Stationers' Company," to his own edition of *The Plays and Poems of William Shakspeare in Ten Volumes*, I, 250–386.

[5] 2 vols. (Oxford, 1930). Chambers covers the subject in his Chapter VIII, Vol. I, "The Problem of Chronology," and acknowledges his debt to Malone, Preface, p. viii.

[6] *The Works of Mr. William Shakespear; in Six Volumes*, I, vi, vii.

[7] *Coleridge's Shakespearean Criticism*, ed. T. M. Raysor.

In the second class I reckon
Midsummer Night's Dream.
As You Like It.
Tempest.
Twelfth Night.[8]

Coleridge goes on to enumerate four periods, thereby anticipating Dowden. In the fourth lecture of his 1811–12 series, Coleridge returned to the problem of chronology, and the reporter had this to say: "As the first of his poems, or rather, amongst the first, he should place the *Love's Labour['s] Lost* together with the *All's Well That Ends Well, Romeo and Juliet, Midsummer Night's Dream, As You Like It, The Tempest, Winter's Tale, Twelfth Night*—all, in short, in which the poet still blends with the dramatist, but in which the dramatist still seems to press forward and never loses his own being in the character he represents to us."[9] I cite *The Tempest* because Malone too had been mistaken in dating it, but when he uncovered contemporary documents more closely suggesting the true date, he published a retraction together with the reasons responsible for his changed opinion—and this incidentally, in 1808, when Coleridge was just beginning to lecture on Shakespeare.[10]

But Coleridge was not interested in the kind of evidence Malone sought. What he brought to bear was something wholly different and certainly no less important. The distinction between Fancy and Imagination was to play a central role in twentieth-century thinking when critics began to grapple for a more exact definition of the way in which words make poetry. Coleridge distinguished between Fancy and Imagination through two quotations from *Venus and Adonis*. Again I cite Raysor, although in a note Raysor himself

[8] Raysor, I, 211–12.
[9] Raysor, II, 67.
[10] Edmond Malone, *An Account of the Incidents from Which The Title and Part of the Story of Shakespeare's Tempest Were Derived, and its True Date Ascertained.*

6

observes, "The famous distinction of fancy and imagination is best studied in chs. iv.–xiii. of B[iographia] L[iteraria], or better, in Shawcross's Introduction to the Oxford edition of this work."[11] But for our purposes what Coleridge says here is adequate:

> Next, we have shewn that he possessed fancy, considered as the faculty of bringing together [images dissimilar in the main by some one point or more of likeness distinguished].
> > Full gently now she takes him by the hand,
> > A lily prison'd in a gaol of snow,
> > Or ivory in an alabaster band;
> > So white a friend engirts so white a foe.
> > > *V. and A.*, 361–364.[12]

Coleridge next proceeds to define imagination:

> Still mounting, we find undoubted proof in his mind of imagination, or the power by which one image or feeling is made to modify many others and by a sort of *fusion to force many into one*. . . . Thus the flight of Adonis from the enamoured goddess in the dusk of the evening—
> > Look! how a bright star shooteth from the sky,
> > So glides he in the night from Venus' eye.
> > > [*V. and A.*, 815–816.][13]

To this couplet Coleridge appends his justly famous explanation of the imagination at work: "How many images and feelings are here brought together without effort and without discord—the beauty of Adonis—the rapidity of his flight—the yearning yet hopelessness of the enamoured gazer—and a shadowy ideal character thrown over the whole."[14]

I have been quoting Coleridge at length not so much for the greatness of his critical insight but to illustrate that his method was

[11] Raysor, I, 188 n.
[12] Raysor, I, 188.
[13] Raysor, I, 188–89.
[14] Raysor, I, 189.

wholly unhistoric—timeless, in that he treated Shakespeare as his contemporary—and therefore different in kind from the habit of mind employed by the great eighteenth-century critics and the Victorian alike. Coleridge knew Malone's work but despaired of its application:

> Various attempts have been made to arrange the plays of Shakespeare, each according to its priority in time, by proofs derived from external documents. How unsuccessful these attempts have been might easily be shown, not only from the widely different result arrived at by men, all deeply versed in the blackletter books, old plays, pamphlets, manuscript records and catalogues of that age, but also from the fallacious and unsatisfactory nature of the facts and assumptions on which the evidence rests.[15]

Coleridge was to be scolded by the Victorians for reasons rather different from those employed in the twentieth century. Leavisites lump him with Bradley to criticize character mongering,[16] but Matthew Arnold reflected the rather different Victorian suspicion of ego gratification divorced from moral or social responsibility. What Arnold distrusted was the passionately indulgent sentimentality running through the entire gamut of romantic rapture.

> What helps it now, that Byron bore,
> With haughty scorn which mock'd the smart,
> Through Europe to the Aetolian shore
> The pageant of his bleeding heart?[17]

Earlier twentieth-century literature indulged its own flair for

---

15 Raysor, I, 208.

16 "During the twentieth-century turn to 'historical' criticism, Coleridge was struck by brickbats, sometimes aimed at him directly but usually ricocheting from the head of A. C. Bradley." Alfred Harbage, Introduction to *Coleridge's Writings on Shakespeare*, ed. Terence Hawkes. "Even though . . . Bradley . . . has gone out of fashion . . . he is still a very potent and mischievous influence." F. R. Leavis, *The Common Pursuit*, p. 137.

17 *Stanzas from the Grande Chartreuse*, ll. 133–36.

bank-clerk Byronism. Mr. Eliot's influential pageant of the bleeding heart (and Eliot was preeminently *the* critic to attempt Arnold's role in our century) may be compared to the mutually exclusive messianic political programs whose consequences we still live with. Engrossment in self seems to have been a characteristic of the age which, among other things, discouraged the tolerance and sense of perspective necessary to dramatic character analysis.

Arnold devoted no essay to Coleridge, while his remarks on Shelley were inspired in the course of reviewing Dowden's *Life*. In truth, Coleridge's criticism often fails to preserve the distinction Matthew Arnold was to emphasize so consistently (at least in his prose) between a man's right to think as he chooses and his obligation to think rightly.

What the Victorians thought of romanticism and Coleridge in particular may be illustrated by the Preface to Aytoun's *Firmilian*, a Victorian satire of egocentricity: "The office of poetry is to exhibit the passions in that state of excitement which distinguishes one from the other."[18] This romantic tendency was precisely what the Victorians had set themselves against. The supposed author of *Firmilian* proceeds with his definition, aiming directly at Coleridge: "Hamlet is said to shadow forth 'Constitutional Irresolution';—my object in Firmilian has been to typify 'Intellect without Principle.' "[19]

Hamlet illustrates the chief weakness of Coleridge's criticism, judgment having been submerged in enthusiasm. Insisting that Shakespeare's judgment was equal to his genius, Coleridge refused to apply any external standard of evaluation. Aytoun ridicules the raptures Coleridge indulges over *Hamlet* conceived in his own image, and even Raysor recognizes the compelling attraction Hamlet exerted: "But it is not unfair to Coleridge to add that his interest in Hamlet was not entirely objective and critical. He felt

[18] W. E. Aytoun, *Firmilian: A "Spasmodic" Tragedy*, pp. vi–vii.
[19] Aytoun, p. vii.

and said that there was something of Hamlet in himself; and his judgment has been almost universally accepted, save by those few vigorous rebels who reverse it, to find Coleridge in his interpretation of Hamlet."[20]

Coleridge encouraged satire by his cloying fulsomeness. He could be as irritating as any one of the later Victorians enraptured over the "Poet." I quote one sentence from a paragraph as famous as it is embarrassing: "Assuredly the Englishman who without reverence, who without a proud and affectionate reverence, can utter the name of Shakespeare, stands disqualified for the office [of critic]."[21]

Coleridge's debt to Schlegel is well documented, but romanticism flourished elsewhere on the Continent before reaching England. Arnold's hostility to certain French indulgences—what he called "French lubricity"—goes back to a time long before the 1870's and is connected with the exaltation of pure passion in France that had been acknowledged in Dr. Johnson's century: "It would be an exaggeration to say that the eighteenth century did not care whether a feeling was labelled 'love' or 'hate' or 'pain' so long as it was sufficiently vivid, but it undoubtedly subordinated these differences to the broad yet vital distinction between *passion* and *stupeur*, and in practice tended to accept the quantitative criterion."[22]

And it is, I believe, no accident that Matthew Arnold, despite the denigration heaped on Johnson by Macaulay, rightly estimated

[20] Raysor, I, xliv.

[21] Raysor, I, 113. Hamlet's conduct is susceptible to far less charitable interpretation than Coleridge's. G. Wilson Knight is usually credited with this change in critical tack; yet T. S. Eliot's 1927 Shakespeare Association lecture, "Shakespeare and the Stoicism of Seneca," contains the following aside: "But even Hamlet, who has made a pretty considerable mess of things, and occasioned the death of at least three innocent people, and two more insignificant ones, dies fairly well pleased with himself." (Ridler, ed., *Shakespeare Criticism 1919–1935* [World Classic], p. 216.)

[22] Martin Turnell, *The Art of French Fiction*, p. 49.

that great man's contribution to English culture. Arnold praised Johnson's prose style in his Preface to *Johnson's Chief Lives of the Poets*.[23] But the principal reason for Arnold's return to Johnson despite the contempt of both Coleridge and Macaulay was the firmness with which Johnson rooted criticism in common morality, offering objections to Shakespeare which Coleridge saw fit to ignore. Johnson's "General Observation" on the character of Bertram in *All's Well* is worth quoting (despite our awareness that Bertram's character is conditioned by the sources from which Shakespeare worked) because his moral center seems to be what we would today classify as Victorian: "I cannot reconcile my heart to Bertram; a man noble without generosity, and young without truth; who marries Helen as a coward and leaves her as a profligate; when she is dead by his unkindness, sneaks home to a second marriage, is accused by a woman whom he has wronged, defends himself by falsehood, and is dismissed to happiness."[24] Coleridge ignores the topic, although in his *Table Talk* Coleridge attempted a whitewash of Bertram's character directed principally at Johnson. Only *Measure for Measure* proved too much for Coleridge: "This play, which is Shakespeare's throughout, is to me the most painful —say rather, the only painful—part of his genuine works."[25]

Keats's criticism, despite the fragmentary nature of his contribution—scattered as it is through his letters—offers the richest possibilities for synthesis. Keats, more than any other romantic poet, realized Coleridge's definition of imagery. He welded familiar objects into new combinations, and for this Murry applied to

[23] London, 1879. "Johnson . . . wrote a prose decidedly modern . . . in spite of superficial differences, the style of our own day" (pp. vii–viii). "The more we study him, the higher . . . will be our esteem for his character" (p. xi). But surprisingly, Arnold seems to have approved Macaulay's *Life*, and included it here, although this slander, contributed to the eighth edition of the *Encyclopædia Britannica* (1856), did much to obscure Johnson's genius.

[24] *Samuel Johnson on Shakespeare*, ed. W. K. Wimsatt, Jr., p. 84.

[25] Raysor, I, 102.

him the epithet "Shakespearean."[26] But Keats's greatness is not fully realized so long as we consider him exclusively a romantic. Keats's greatest contribution was his awareness of romantic limitation. One of the many achievements of his *Ode* on Truth and Beauty was the marriage of beauty, the specific romantic contribution, with truth, which had been the abiding concern of Dr. Johnson: "The business of a poet . . . is to examine, not the individual, but the species; to remark general properties and large appearances: he does not number the streaks of the tulip, or describe the different shades of verdure of the forest."[27] Coleridge's borrowings were not restricted to Schlegel, and romanticism owes Johnson more than is acknowledged:

> I adopt with full faith the principle of Aristotle, that poetry as poetry is essentially *ideal*, that it avoids and excludes all *accident*; that its apparent individualities of rank, character, or occupation must be *representative* of a class; and that the *persons* of poetry must be clothed with generic attributes, with the *common* attributes of the class: not with such as one gifted individual might possibly possess, but such as from his situation it is most probable before-hand that he *would* possess.[28]

Both *Hyperion* and *The Fall of Hyperion* are unsuccessful attempts to fuse classic truth with romantic perception, to work out the scheme suggested by his *Ode on a Grecian Urn*.

Since Keats, toward the end of his brief working life, began to realize the limitations of immediate perception or imagination, his reliance on the "holiness of the Heart's affections,"[29] it is especially

---

[26] John Middleton Murry, *Keats and Shakespeare* (1925).

[27] *Rasselas*, Ch. X.

[28] *Biographia Literaria*, ed. J. Shawcross, II, 33–34.

[29] *The Letters of John Keats*, ed. Hyder Edward Rollins, I, 184. Most of the catch phrases that popularly define Keats as a romantic come from his early letters. Keats grew up fast, and the richness of his later correspondence is astounding. The phrase I have quoted comes from a letter catalogued No. 43 out of a total of 320 items, mostly by Keats.

unfortunate that Keats misunderstood Johnson's method. He seems never to have had any sympathy for Johnson. Caroline Spurgeon reproduced several plates from Keats's copy of Shakespeare; beneath a note of Dr. Johnson's on *The Winter's Tale*, Keats had scribbled " 'lo fool again'!"[30] But Johnson's sense of truth, embedded in the perceptions of his common reader, would have stood Keats in good stead when he tried to define the true as something more than "What the imagination seizes as Beauty."[31]

In one of his great letters, Keats hints at the method to be employed in establishing the order of Shakespeare's plays. Writing to his brother on February 19, 1819, he concludes a paragraph in that marvelous journal letter:

> . . . and above all that they are very shallow people who take every thing literal. A Man's life of any worth is a continual allegory—and very few eyes can see the Mystery of his life—a life like the scriptures, figurative—which such people can no more make out than they can the hebrew Bible. Lord Byron cuts a figure—but he is not figurative—Shakespeare led a life of Allegory; his works are the comments on it—."[32]

This is so different from Malone's method as to constitute a difference in kind—the difference between Imagination and Fancy, about which Coleridge spoke. "His works are the comments on a life of allegory." Malone would have been unable to come to terms with a statement like that. "How do you document it?" he might have asked. Malone's question would have been appropriate to a member in good standing of the New Shakspere Society.

[30] This reflects the flavor of Keats's criticism of Johnson throughout. (Caroline F. E. Spurgeon, *Keats's Shakespeare: A Descriptive Study*, pp. 29–32, plates 6–10).

[31] "I am certain of nothing but of the holiness of the Heart's affections and the truth of Imagination—What the imagination seizes as Beauty must be truth—whether it existed before or not—for I have the same Idea of all our Passions as of Love they are all in their sublime, creative of essential Beauty." (Rollins, I, 184.) For Coleridge and Keats Imagination is a creative faculty.

[32] Rollins, II, 67.

13

Our analysis, which has hitherto been qualitative, must become quantitative; ... the test ... is this: "Can you say, not only of what kind, but how much? If you cannot weigh, measure, number your results, however you may be convinced yourself, you must not hope to convince others, or claim the position of an investigator; you are merely a guessor, a propounder of hypotheses."[33]

Significantly, Keats did not bother to acquire the Malone edition of Shakespeare. Yet Keats's comment, like Coleridge's catalogue, looks forward, surprisingly, to Edward Dowden, who in 1875 was vastly to popularize the notion that Shakespeare's plays reflect four periods through which he passed in the course of his mortal existence.

Dowden has of course been in disfavor since Lytton Strachey's essay of 1904,[34] his critical disrepute strengthened by the Leavis diatribes directed against the Bradley we have left behind.[35] This disdain for character analysis, a revulsion against the cult of personality, corresponds to the destruction of individuality in other arts as well, and is distinctly a late-nineteenth-century reaction against the age then ending. Thus the impressionists and Picasso began eroding the visual representation of reality at about the same time, and not much later atonal music began deliberately to destroy the accustomed notion of sound.

Coleridge's investigation of imagination, the fresh combinations of metaphor unstaled by eighteenth-century usage, put into prose his generation's poetic achievement. This new combination of imagery is what Wordsworth and Keats accomplished at their

[33] New Shakspere Society, *Transactions 1874*, p. 2.

[34] "Shakespeare's Final Period," *Independent Review*, III (Aug. 1904), 405–18. Reprinted in Strachey's *Books and Characters*. Dowden lived until 1913, active to the last.

[35] "*The Tempest* is by more general agreement a masterpiece than *The Winter's Tale* . . . Lytton Strachey, in his essay on 'Shakespeare's Final Period' . . . gives us an opening . . ." (Anne Ridler, *Shakespeare Criticism 1935–1960*, p. 139). Strachey was no forerunner of the new criticism, but he was critical of the Victorian assumption about Shakespeare's ultimate serenity.

14

best, principally in poetry but in their critical fragments also, brief and dazzling. I have in mind their letters, but even Wordsworth's essays seem not so much pieces of coherent exposition as a series of discrete particles like mosaic art. Yet the center of Victorian criticism derives from an earlier generation, and—to anticipate— the strength of modern criticism lies in the fusion of Victorian method and romantic insight, its principal limitation in the abandonment of Victorian commitment.

Malone brought to criticism patience, a sharp eye, and scrupulous methods of investigation. He formulated habits of procedure on which we pride ourselves today. Is the document genuine? Where does it belong? What void in our history of Shakespeare studies does it help fill?

Johnson's contribution, grounded in moral judgment, seems more important today than Malone's emphasis on historical method, "For the same reason that an eagle is not so fine a thing as a truth," to quote one of Keats's mature letters.[36] Both are to reappear in Victorian criticism and together constitute its strength. The romantics cared for neither Malone nor Johnson, but, fortunately, Johnson is no longer scanted by glib readers of Macaulay's *Britannica* article. Bertrand Bronson's *Johnson Agonistes*[37] inaugurated this changing estimate, and he is given his due in Walter Jackson Bate's *The Achievement of Samuel Johnson.*[38]

Dr. Johnson, with patient trust in the common reader, distilled his own fervent intensity out of criticism to approach with judicial calm and magisterial pose the "Poet of Nature." For this Keats wrote " 'lo fool again'!" in his copy of Shakespeare, and for this

[36] Rollins, II, 81.
[37] Cambridge, 1946. First published in 1944 by the University of California Press as *Johnson and Boswell.*
[38] New York, 1955. American book collectors, like R. B. Adam and A. Edward Newton, deserve an honorable footnote for having recognized Johnson a generation before the scholars. Not until 1965 did S. C. Roberts, who loved Johnson, rewrite Macaulay for the *Britannica.*

we tend to think of him as a rationalist setting up the easy comparison of a stodgy, blunt man opposed by the earnest sympathy of Coleridge. But the gifted critic entertains contrarieties, and each generation selects what is needful to its search for truth. Thus something quite unexpected, like the exposed document in Poe's *Purloined Letter*, may lie unobserved to general scrutiny.

In her introduction to *Shakespeare Criticism 1919–1935*, Anne Ridler quotes with pleased surprise Johnson's memorable phrase about the relativity of time: "Time is, of all modes of existence, most obsequious to the imagination."[39] The sense of her quotation is an astounded and grudged surprise that the rational Johnson could apply so striking and apposite an image. But any ten lines from *The Vanity of Human Wishes* discloses an artist despairing at the malignity of envious and calumniating time. All through his working life Johnson had what we would call a Proustian sense of time which he tried painfully to adjust to the norms of his society. Like Swinburne, whose criticism is richer and more relevant than the early twentieth century realized, he would have been sympathetic to the distortions of time employed by G. Wilson Knight.[40] Manipulation of the fourth dimension has become a

[39] Page viii.

[40] Helen Gardner, in *The Business of Criticism*, reprints an essay entitled "The Historical Approach," which touches several aspects of Johnson's greatness. "Johnson also took the historical in his stride. He had far more historical knowledge than Dryden, and, with his work as lexicographer and editor behind him, is the patron of all scholar-critics, as Dryden is the patron of all men of letters and of the poet turned critic. But their fundamental position is the same." She then quotes the opening of Johnson's note on *Macbeth*: "In order to make a true estimate of the abilities and merit of a writer, it is always necessary to examine the genius of his age, and the opinions of his contemporaries." This habit of mind she contrasts with Coleridge: "Criticism after Coleridge, which accepts as axiomatic the integrity of a work of art as the product of a creative imagination, cannot make this distinction between the kernel of eternal moral truth and the shell of outmoded belief. . . . The greatest example of a fundamentally unhistoric approach is Coleridge's treatment of *Hamlet*." (Pp. 26–29.) Miss Gardner does not connect Johnson and the Victorian historical tradition.

16

respectable activity in our century, and one to which the historical critic easily accommodates himself. Swinburne died about the time Freud and Einstein were making it all acceptable.[41]

[41] G. Wilson Knight's criticism, what he calls "spatial analysis," finds its Victorian antecedent in Swinburne. E. A. Abbott, author of *A Shakespearian Grammar*, published anonymously *Flatland: A Romance of Many Dimensions*, a science-fiction fantasy which plays with distortions of the time dimension. Unfortunately, he does not bring this habit of mind to his very rational and detailed book on Shakespeare. So diverse a trio as Knight, Dr. Johnson, and Dame Helen Gardner—but not Swinburne, despite the mealy piety alleged against Victorian critics—all introduced a measure of Christian morality into their criticism. To good advantage, my point is only to remark another stereotype of the post-Victorian age.

THE DATE OF AN ACTION, then, signifies nothing: the action itself, its selection and construction, this is what is all-important. This the Greeks understood far more clearly than we do. . . . They regarded the whole; we regard the parts. With them, the action predominated over the expression of it; with us, the expression predominates over the action. . . . We have poems which seem to exist merely for the sake of single lines and passages; not for the sake of producing any total impression. . . . The confusion of the present times is great, the multitude of voices counselling different things bewildering, the number of existing works capable of attracting a young writer's attention and of becoming his models, immense. . . . Foremost among these models for the English writer stands Shakespeare. . . . He has not the severe and scrupulous self-restraint of the ancients, partly, no doubt, because he had a far less cultivated and exacting audience. He has indeed a far wider range than they had, a far richer fertility of thought; in this respect he rises above them. In his strong conception of his subject, in the genuine way in which he is penetrated with it, he resembles them, and is unlike the moderns. But in the accurate limitation of it, the conscientious rejection of superfluities, the simple and rigorous development of it from the first line of his work to the last, he falls below them, and comes nearer to the moderns. . . . He is therefore a less safe model; for what he has of his own is personal, and inseparable from his own rich nature; it may be imitated and exaggerated, it cannot be learned or applied as an art.

—Preface to *Poems* (1853) in Matthew Arnold,
On the Classical Tradition

the victorian method

The common notion of Victorian criticism of Shakespeare is unfortunately still one of transcendental gush over the "Poet" interspersed with romantic glimpses of Anne Hathaway's cottage, a quarter-mile down the road at Shottery. This cozy domestic scene is familiar to us in engravings and etchings that adorned editions of Shakespeare all through our period from Charles Knight's *Pictorial Shakespeare*[1] to the Henry Irving Shakespeare,[2] when whatever was characteristically Victorian had become diffused into the *fin de siècle* atmosphere now designated Edwardian.

F. E. Halliday, with more charity than most modern critics, places the origin of this distortion in a period preceding the Victorian:

> In England the impact of the great Romantic critics was twofold, both good and bad; on the one hand they succeeded in communicating to others something of the ecstacy they experienced themselves in their discovery of Shakespeare, on the other they supplied later critics with a vicious model, and the nineteenth century resounds with what Croce calls *exclamatory* criticism, "which instead of understanding a poet in his particularity, his finite-infinity, drowns him beneath a flood of superlatives." Few people, not even Voltaire, had ever questioned Shakespeare's genius; on the other hand, until about 1770 few people had admitted his art; but when Coleridge had demonstrated that his art was as great as, if not greater than, his genius, what could there be left to find fault

---

[1] 8 vols. (London, 1843).
[2] H. Irving, F. A. Marshall, *Henry Irving Edition.*

with? "Others abide our question," Arnold sang, but Shakespeare was beyond criticism, and there was nothing left for the critics but to adore and see who could shout his adulation the loudest.[3]

Halliday overlooks Arnold's astringency and the uncanny modernity of a critic writing in 1853 about poems which exist "for the sake of single lines and passages; not for the sake of producing any total impression." Shakespeare's relation to a problem with us today is still a topic worth investigating. Halliday proceeds with a general indictment: "The Victorians had failed to develop the creative criticism of Coleridge in the direction that he had indicated. Instead of integrating the man and his work they were divorcing them and taking them to pieces; instead of pursuing the secret of the organic growth of the plays they were bandying conventional and uncritical hyperbole."[4]

The Victorians did not develop in the direction Coleridge indicated, but they left us a scientific tradition of great breadth on which twentieth-century "creative" criticism was once again to build. With true revolutionary ardor, some critics managed to build with Victorian capital while strenuously repudiating the existence of any debt. Henri Fluchère, whose *Shakespeare* comes to us warmly recommended by T. S. Eliot, sums up the Victorians in a single paragraph:

> There has also been a reaction against those nineteenth-century critics who used Shakespeare merely as a splendid pretext for writing about themselves, of whom the Romantics Hazlitt, Lamb and, later, Swinburne were the most notable. Brilliant writers in their different ways, moving panegyrists, they told the stories at secondhand, copying the fine series of Shakespeare's pictures, the "incomparable gallery" of heroes and heroines over whom they shed pitying tears. Their attitude is that of disciples and friends who dole out their emotion in well-timed essays full of the prestige of

[3] *Shakespeare and His Critics*, p. 24.
[4] F. E. Halliday, p. 27.

their name and style: they for long stereotyped the "right" attitude and formulas to be adopted towards "The Bard." In so doing they tell us more about themselves and their own day than about Shakespeare. But, apart from Coleridge who remains a great critic, the critical importance of these essays is largely negligible.[5]

In his concluding section, Fluchère proceeds to organize the plays along the lines proposed by G. G. Gervinus of Heidelberg and popularized in England by F. J. Furnivall and the New Shakspere Society, founded in 1873. (The worth of Swinburne's Shakespeare criticism is discussed in my next chapter.)

The first of the Oxford World Classics on Shakespeare criticism (1916), an invaluable barometer to critical attitudes of the early twentieth century, disposed of Victorian critics (defined by the editor, D. Nichol Smith, as men writing after Carlyle in 1840 through Bradley's great lectures published as *Shakespearean Tragedy* in 1904) in a single concluding paragraph:

> Carlyle's paean is a fitting climax to the passages in this volume. Subsequent criticism to the end of the century shows no conspicuous change in attitude and purpose. The three books which stand out prominently are Edward Dowden's *Shakspere, His Mind and Art* (1874); Swinburne's *Study of Shakespeare* (1880); and A. C. Bradley's *Shakespearean Tragedy*. Though not published till 1904, Mr. Bradley's penetrative analysis of the four chief tragedies is the last great representative of nineteenth-century criticism, and nothing better in its kind need be expected. It continues the traditions inaugurated by Whately and Morgann, and established by Coleridge and Hazlitt. A clear break with these traditions is to be found already in the criticism of the twentieth century.[6]

Smith himself was one of the last critics to treat Bradley with respect before the onslaught of bright young men began in the

[5] London, 1953, pp. 10–11.
[6] D. Nichol Smith, ed., *Shakespeare Criticism: A Selection, 1623–1840*, p. xxi.

1920's. In this chapter I hope to illustrate another school of Victorian criticism developing independently of Smith's three representative Victorian critics and in the teeth of Swinburne's ferocious opposition.

The gush, associated with Dowden, Swinburne, and often Bradley too, goes back at least as far as Coleridge, although he is probably indebted to one of his unacknowledged Continental sources, probably German—Schlegel or Goethe perhaps. Coleridge defends himself at length against charges of cribbing Schlegel's notes; I shall quote instead Wilhelm Meister delivering his impression of Hamlet:

> A lovely, pure, noble, and most moral nature, without the strength of nerve which forms a hero, sinks beneath a burden it cannot bear and must not cast away. All duties are holy for him: the present is too hard. Impossibilities have been required of him— not in themselves impossibilities, but such for him. He winds and turns, and torments himself; he advances and recoils; is ever put in mind, ever puts himself in mind; at last does all but lose his purpose from his thoughts, yet still without recovering his peace of mind.[7]

This is the very Coleridge given us by William Hazlitt in "My First Acquaintance with Poets" down to the "winding walk": "I observed that he continually crossed me on the way by shifting from one side of the footpath to the other. This struck me as an odd movement; but I did not at that time connect it with any instability of purpose or involuntary change of principle, as I have done since. He seemed unable to keep on in a straight line."[8]

Since a fundamentally uncritical attitude is attributed by most twentieth-century commentators to their Victorian predecessors, it

---

[7] J. W. von Goethe, *Wilhelm Meister's Apprenticeship* (Berlin, 1795), Carlyle's translation of 1824. Final paragraph, Book IV, Ch. XIII.

[8] *Selected Essays of William Hazlitt*, ed. Geoffrey Keynes (London, 1930), p. 509. First appeared in *The Liberal*, April, 1823.

seems useful to elaborate Halliday's observation and begin finding the principal stream from which that criticism flowed. More than Childe Harold, more than Werther, more than René himself, Coleridge, by what he did, what he was, and what he failed to become, represents that inexhaustible discontent, fragmentation, and endless regret the chords of which, as Matthew Arnold so appositely observed, sound through all our modern literature.

It is also a commonplace to attribute method and its rational application to the Victorian age. This is one of the significant differences between our period and the preceding one. Watt's steam engine and Arkwright's spinning jenny are technically part of the eighteenth century, but their full application rests with the nineteenth.[9] Steam plied the railroads, and new power-driven factories came to dominate an increasingly industrial society. The entire century is dominated by industrialization. In the 1840's, the factory system stirred independent reformers like Carlyle and Dickens; near the century's close, it summoned the cooperative response of Toynbee Hall and the Independent Labour party.

Habits of industry and cooperative organization affected scholarly production too. The work of Malone and Steevens was broadened immensely by men equipped to cope with the cooperative apparatus implicit in factory organization. By applying scientific method to the insight of earlier scholars, they strengthened the foundations upon which modern textual critics were to build. Most of this work was characteristically unglamorous but necessary, each fact adding to the mosaic of historical perspective upon

[9] "Fortunately we are now permitted to use the phrase the 'Industrial Revolution' for what happened in Britain between 1770 and about 1840. Economic historians in the recent past have been rather diffident about allowing us to use those words. They have had good reason for this. Very often in history when what seems to a superficial view to be a complete revolution is more closely studied it becomes clear that the change has been neither so unprecedented nor so complete as had been imagined." G. Kitson Clark, *The Making of Victorian England*, p. 84.

23

which our own century prizes itself. E. K. Chambers, the ripest of historical scholars, whose two volumes on Shakespeare are by common consent the foundation of whatever is written today,[10] acknowledged in an earlier work his debt to the Victorians: "The work of gathering together miscellaneous documents and studies passed from *The Shakespeare Society's Papers* (1844–49) to the *Transactions of the New Shakspere Society* (1874–92), and is now carried on by the *Collections* (1907–13) of the *Malone Society*."[11]

The industrialization of Shakespeare studies has not yet exhausted itself. Charlton Hinman did not develop his "collation machine" (the phrase is his own) until after World War II.

> Beginning just after the Second World War I had undertaken to devise a means of speeding up accurate collation, to develop an instrument with which one man might collate the Folger Folios within a few years' time. My efforts were not immediately rewarded, but by the end of 1952, after much trial and error, I had succeeded in constructing such an instrument—and had begun to collate the Folger collection of First Folios.[12]

This has the flavor of a Victorian inventor describing a new process designed to revolutionize some branch of commerce. As the railroad did more than accelerate travel by coach, and the automobile much more than improve on the railroad, so Hinman's machine promises much more than a mere speedup of collation. "The bulk of the evidence used to reconstruct the printing of the First Folio, and also most of the techniques developed to exploit this evidence, are wholly new."[13]

Hinman's apparatus may be new, but the technique, it seems to me, was articulated by two Victorian bibliographers who were

[10] *William Shakespeare: A Study of Facts and Problems.*

[11] *The Elizabethan Stage*, I, xvi.

[12] Charlton Hinman, *The Printing and Proof-Reading of the First Folio of Shakespeare*, p. 8.

[13] Hinman, p. 13.

24

among the first incunabulists: Henry Bradshaw (1831–86) and Robert Proctor (1866–1903). Hinman is applying Bradshaw's "natural-history order," devised to deal with incunabula to the seventeenth century. Although Hinman is far more detailed than any of his predecessors, the first man to apply Bradshaw to Shakespeare was, I think, Alfred W. Pollard (1859–1944), whose *Shakespeare Folios and Quartos: A Study in the Bibliography of Shakespeare's Plays, 1594–1685* appeared in 1909. Bradshaw, like Pollard, was a friend of F. J. Furnivall, founder of the New Shakspere Society, and it is a great pity Furnivall was unable to involve Bradshaw in the society. Bradshaw's learning and caution would have advanced Shakespeare bibliography half a century and perhaps have eliminated the Furnivall-Swinburne controversy, a scholarly dispute of almost unparalleled virulence that enlivened the literary scene in the late 1870's. (Pollard did not then know Furnivall.) Proctor, who extended Bradshaw's work and laid the foundation for the British Museum catalogue of fifteenth-century books, disappeared on an Alpine climb—that Victorian equivalent of the bullfight—before his career was really under way.

It is true that the origin of an historical method, like the Industrial Revolution itself, can be put back even earlier than Malone. In a turn-of-the-century work, D. Nichol Smith suggested just that:

> After the publication of Farmer's *Essay* [*on the Learning of Shakespeare*] there was a change in the character of the editions of Shakespeare. Farmer is the forerunner of Steevens and Malone . . . it is doubtful if any later editor has contributed as much as either of them did to elucidation of Shakespeare's text. They have been oftener borrowed from than has been admitted, and many a learned note of later date may be found in germ in their editions.[14]

[14] D. Nichol Smith, ed., *Eighteenth-Century Essays on Shakespeare*, pp. xxvii–xxviii. First published in 1903.

25

But he cites a single individual, two or three at most, and the method toward which they were groping was not fully exploited by any group of men working cooperatively, or at least trying to, before the Victorian period.

Collier's Shakespeare Society was the first of these learned bodies cited by Chambers in his Preface to *The Elizabeth Stage*. Founded in 1840, it came to an end in 1853 when Collier's forgeries were being exposed in the text of Samuel Weller Singer's *The Text of Shakespeare Vindicated from the Interpolations and Corruptions Advocated by John Payne Collier Esq. in His Notes and Emendations*—a self-explanatory title.[15] But the council Collier set up in 1840 included Victorian scholars like the publisher Charles Knight, J. O. Halliwell,[16] and the Reverend Alexander Dyce, who died in 1869 but whose work was important throughout the century. Significantly, Halliwell and other younger men who were active in the more influential New Shakspere Society (1873–94) engaged principally in the expansion and classification of knowledge, not the rapturous interpretation we now associate with their century.

None of the three Victorians mentioned by Smith—Dowden, Swinburne, or Bradley—is indebted to this critical tradition, although Dowden applied certain research developed by the New Shakspere Society to corroborate his speculative opinions. The spelling is deliberate—F. J. Furnivall insisted that scholarly research demands "Shakspere." This was a point of sore contention in the second half of the century, and men generally inclined to

---

[15] London, 1853. Singer utilized the occasion to bring out a revised edition of his ten-volume Shakespeare that had first appeared in 1826.

[16] Halliwell (later Halliwell-Phillipps) (1820–89), a Cambridge man like most who figure in this chapter, was educated first at Trinity, then Jesus, although he went down in 1840 without a degree. Trinity was an excellent college for incipient Shakespeareans since it boasted Capell's Shakespeare collection. For details, see the *Catalogue of the Books Presented by Edward Capell to the Library of Trinity College in Cambridge*, ed. W. W. Greg.

science went along with him. Swinburne, as might well be expected, furiously opposed this variant spelling of the poet's name as pedantic nonsense.

Notwithstanding obvious personal irregularities, Collier represents in his own person much of this Victorian perspective. He is also a bridge back to Coleridge; as a younger man, he first came into prominence taking down transcripts of Coleridge's lectures. But despite his close acquaintance with romantic interpretation, he is another of the Victorians to whom F. E. Halliday might have pointed as having failed to develop in the direction Coleridge had indicated. Collier's forgeries reflect a personal instability not to be confused with some of Coleridge's vagaries.

Forgery seems to have been endemic in the nineteenth century. Young Halliwell was accused of stealing manuscripts from his college library (Trinity, Cambridge), the kind of thing T. J. Wise compounded with forgery, possibly to escape detection, near the century's close. Halliwell's obscure youth and rise to respectability disclose interesting parallels with Wise's career.[17]

Collier's failure to develop according to romantic precept is significant of the early Victorian age and something he shares with Tennyson, who did not develop in the direction of Keats (*The Palace of Art* in the volume of 1832 represents the turning point here). Similarly, Browning realized that Shelley was an unacceptable model, however deep the strain of admiration ran.

Collier's contribution is naturally obscured by the forgeries in which he indulged; but in addition to founding the first learned society, the forefather of our own Shakespeare Association of

---

[17] Alderman Pariser of Manchester, the Wise specialist, wrote me: "I think it likely that Wise was acquainted with Halliwell-Phillipps but I do not recollect ever seeing any evidence of this. The introduction could have been made by Furnivall as you suggest, and Wise in his early days would doubtless have greatly valued an acquaintance with a man of Halliwell-Phillipps' eminence. . . . I also think it likely Wise would have known of Halliwell-Phillipps' thefts." (Personal communication, letter, August 6, 1964)

America, he deserves credit for at least one other scholarly contribution. In 1831 he published *The History of English Dramatic Poetry to the Time of Shakespeare: And Annals of the Stage to the Restoration.*[18] The value of this history is generously acknowledged by A. W. Ward on the first page of his *History of English Dramatic Literature to the Death of Queen Anne* (1899); Chambers, in his *Elizabethan Stage*, acknowledges his own debt to Ward. In addition to this very thorough historical survey, Collier emphasizes a strain in the drama which is currently in the process of being discovered. He writes copiously on the miracle play, explaining that this coarse spectacle is the "source and foundation of our national drama."[19] This connection is being remade in our day largely, I believe, as a result of the massive and detailed analysis of Western literature in Eric Auerbach's *Mimesis.*[20]

Throughout the 1830's and 1840's, Collier was fabricating and unearthing old documents which secure Shakespeare more closely to his time and place in the history of England. His Shakespeare Society first printed Dyce's edition of *Sir Thomas More*, and Peter Cunningham's *Extracts from the Accounts of the Revels at Court*, both of which still excite scholarly curiosity. Collier was far from solitary. The Reverend Alexander Dyce, a scholar in the Malone tradition, was editing manuscripts all through the 1830's and 1840's. His Skelton of 1843 helped bring back that early poet from obscurity; in 1857, he edited Shakespeare. But his principal contribution is the *Glossary* of 1864. The great Shakespeare dictionaries are all products of Victorian scholarship. Schmidt's *Shakespeare-Lexicon* appeared in 1874–75; Bartlett's *Concordance*, in 1894. Thus the three countries principally identified with Shakespeare created these basic tools of reference within a generation.

[18] 3 vols. (London, 1831).
[19] Preface, I, ix.
[20] Princeton, 1953.

Collier's history was dedicated to the book-collecting sixth Duke of Devonshire (1790–1858). His discoveries earned him the post of librarian to the duke, when access to Bridgewater Library (containing the papers of Thomas Egerton, Lord Ellesmere [ca. 1540–1617]) further tempted Collier to concoct his evidence and fabricate Elizabethan documents which might be of interest to the Victorian public. He was granted a civil list pension of a hundred pounds in 1850, and his society came to an end in 1853; but Halliwell, who had exposed some of Collier's forgeries and was to make trouble for Furnivall's New Shakspere Society some thirty years later, continued this strain of research until his death in 1889. Oddly, Halliwell became less bold as his life and the century wore on. His *Life of Shakespeare* in 1848, published at the age of twenty-eight, contains some speculation; his *Outlines of the Life of Shakespeare*, published in 1881 and revised continuously until his death in 1889, attempts strenuously to exclude interpretation while searching for facts which contain the only clues to truth.

In 1863, the *Cambridge Shakespeare*, edited by Clarke, Glover and Wright, was begun. Completed in 1866, this nine-volume standard edition was the basis of the *Globe* numbered-line text (1864),[21] still used by scholars.[22] In the preface to *The Shakespeare First Folio*, W. W. Greg observes almost as a matter of course that "All references to Shakespeare's plays are to be the act, scene, and line numbering of the Globe edition. . . ."[23]

In the editing of Shakespeare, the twentieth century naturally has had substantial revisions to make. But these do not consist of revising Victorian enthusiasm. In this specialized and technical field, our own bibliographical experts attempted quite the reverse. I cite Greg's *The Shakespeare First Folio* because of his pre-

[21] The year 1864 also saw Lionel Booth's facsimile reprint of the First Folio, no errors having been discovered in the ensuing century.

[22] The *Globe* provided line numbering for Abbott's *Shakespearian Grammar*, Schmidt's *Shakespeare-Lexicon*, and Bartlett's *Concordance*.

[23] Oxford, 1955, p. v.

eminence among Shakespeare bibliographers and because his Preface states that this work is to be a summation of mid-twentieth-century scholarship: "The work makes no pretence to originality. All I have tried to do is to set out the evidence and summarize on each point under discussion the view now generally held by scholars."[24]

In his chapter entitled "Editorial Problems I," Greg set out to explain how wrong Victorian editors had been to mistrust the Quarto volumes which preceded the First Folio of 1623. He traces in great detail the reasons why scholars now believe there is sufficient reason to credit these Quartos and to discount Victorian skepticism. Much of this credit belongs to the early-twentieth-century scholar Alfred W. Pollard. Greg observes, "The great stimulus to research afforded by Pollard's work, releasing students as it did from the quagmire of nineteenth-century despondency, [concerning the authenticity of copy] has resulted, during the last forty years, in much investigation into the nature of particular texts, which is in the end the only way in which we can hope to answer the question."[25]

The principal Victorian culprit cited by Greg in this chapter, Sir Sidney Lee, was born in the watershed year 1859 and can best be designated as late Victorian.[26] Elsewhere in this chapter, Greg acknowledged that mistrust of the Quartos was not a nineteenth-century innovation and that the great eighteenth-century editors concurred in deprecating them. He also observed that Halliwell, active in both Shakespeare societies, fully recognized their value. Since Lee's observations in the introduction to his facsimile edition of the First Folio[27] are taken as the epitome of Victorian scholar-

[24] Greg, p. v.   [25] Greg, p. 92.
[26] The year 1859 saw the publication of Darwin's *Origin of Species*, Fitz-Gerald's *Rubáiyát*, George Eliot's *Adam Bede*, Meredith's *Richard Feverel*, Mill's *On Liberty*, the first edition of Samuel Smiles' *Self-Help*, and the first four of Tennyson's *Idylls*.
[27] Oxford, 1902.

ship and because his critical attitude is confined by the twentieth-century critics to the nineteenth, it seems fair to quote Greg once more:

> Lee's pronouncement represents, if in an exaggerated form, the view taken by most Shakesperian critics half a century ago, a view based ultimately on the misunderstanding of the words of Heminge and Condell fostered by *the great authority of Malone.*[28] The true meaning of what they wrote was pointed out as early as 1859 by Tycho Mommsen in the introduction to his parallel-text edition of *Romeo and Juliet,* and again by J. O. Halliwell in his *Outline of the Life of Shakespeare* published in 1887, but was ignored by most critics. It was not till in 1909 Pollard raised the banner of revolt against two centuries of pessimism, and linked the correct interpretation of the passage in the address with a fresh insistence on and definition of the distinction between what he named the "good" and the "bad" quartos, that serious attention became focused upon this important issue.[29]

If Bradshaw or Proctor had worked on Shakespeare instead of incunabula, modern bibliography would have begun long before 1909 and perhaps no "banner" need have been raised. Pollard knew Bradshaw's essays, worked with Furnivall and Proctor, and wrote the memoir of Proctor that prefaced the collected edition of Proctor's *Bibliographical Essays* in 1905. The work Greg is referring to as having "raised the banner of revolt against two centuries of pessimism" is Pollard's *Shakespeare Folios and Quartos.*[30] This is the first study I have found to apply the techniques of incunabula bibliography to Shakespeare. Pollard's way of attacking the problem goes through Proctor to Bradshaw and, indeed, back to Bradshaw's mentor J. W. Holtrop, whose *Monuments typographiques des Pays-Bas au quinzième siècle* (HMT) began

---

[28] My italics.

[29] Greg, p. 88. Many years before Pollard, Swinburne was exuberantly attacking Lee's scholarship in the columns of the *Athenaeum.*

[30] London, 1909.

appearing around mid-century. Dating can be highly selective; Pollard and Lee were both born in 1859, yet no one calls Pollard Victorian!

Baiting the Victorians is still a popular academic sport. Writing on *Macbeth*, Cleanth Brooks quotes some famous lines spoken by the murderer shortly after his crime:

> Here lay Duncan,
> His silver skin lac'd with his golden blood;
> And his gash'd stabs, look'd like a breach in nature
> For ruin's wasteful entrance: there, the murderers,
> Steep'd in the colours of their trade, their daggers
> Unmannerly breech'd with gore . . .

Brooks continues:

> It is amusing to watch the textual critics, particularly those of the eighteenth century, fight a stubborn rearguard action against the acceptance of "breech'd."[31]

His final example of obtuseness in the face of irony and paradox is, of course, a Victorian, and Brooks concludes his paragraph on the denseness of all preceding critics as follows:

> *The Shakespeare Glossary* defines "breech'd" as meaning "covered as with breeches," and thus leaves the poet committed to a reading which must still shock the average reader as much as it shocked that nineteenth-century critic who pronounced upon it as follows: "A metaphor must not be far-fetched nor dwell upon the details of the disgusting picture, as in these lines. There is little, and that far-fetched, similarity between *gold lace* and *blood*, or between *bloody daggers* and *breech'd legs*. The slightness of the similarity, recalling the greatness of the dissimilarity, disgusts us with the attempted comparison."[32]

The nineteenth-century critic is Edwin A. Abbott, D.D., head-

---

[31] *The Well Wrought Urn*, p. 28.
[32] Page 29.

master of the City of London School. Brooks is quoting *A Shake-spearian Grammar*,[33] but he has omitted the critical last sentence in Abbott's paragraph: "Language so forced is only appropriate in the mouth of a conscious murderer dissembling guilt."

Abbott is another in the catalogue of Victorian systematizers. The first sentences of his Preface to the first edition explain what he set out to do:

> The object of this work is to furnish students of Shakespeare and Bacon[34] with a short systematic account of some points of differ-ence between Elizabethan syntax and our own. The *words* of these authors present but little difficulty. They can be understood from glossaries, and, even without such aid, a little reflection and attention to the context will generally enable us to hit the mean-ing. But the *differences of idiom* are more perplexing. They are more frequent than mere verbal difficulties, and they are less ob-vious and noticeable. But it need hardly be said, that if we allow ourselves to fancy we are studying Shakespeare critically, when we have not noticed and cannot explain the simplest Shakespearian idiom, we are in danger of seriously lowering our standard of accurate study, and so far from training we are untraining our understanding.[35]

Abbott then goes on to reduce Shakespearean grammar into 529 headings beginning with "Adjectives" and concluding with "Good and Bad Metaphors." It is from the latter, subsection 3, that Brooks begins his quotation, "A metaphor must not be far-fetched."

[33] E. A. Abbott, *A Shakespearian Grammar: An Attempt to Illustrate Some of the Differences between Elizabethan and Modern English* (London, 1883), p. 437. 1st ed., 1869.

[34] Bacon is another key Elizabethan rediscovered by the nineteenth century, and sometimes merged with Shakespeare. James Spedding, who wrote several papers on Shakespeare, was principally engaged in reintroducing Bacon to the Victorian world of letters.

[35] Abbott, p. 437.

33

Abbott has tried to reduce all Shakespeare to rule, and to circumscribe his imagination within the categories he has created for this purpose. Most of the 529 headings deal with the explication of terms no longer clear. Heading 232, selected almost at random, is still useful to the reader who does not often encounter the pronoun "thou":

> Thou is generally used by a master to a servant, but not always. Being the appropriate address to a servant, it is used in confidential and good-humoured utterances, but a master finding fault often resorts to the unfamiliar *you* (much as Caesar cut his soldiers to the heart by giving them the respectful title of Quirites). Thus Valentine uses *you* to Speed in *T.G. of V.* ii. I. 1–17, and *thou, Ib.* 47–69. Compare
>
> "*Val. Go to, sir*: tell me, do *you* know madam Silvia?"—*Ib.* 14. with
> "*Val.* But tell me: dost *thou* know my lady Silvia?"—*Ib. 44.*[36]

Fortunately, Abbott's book is no literary curiosity. Almost every editor of the Arden Shakespeare, currently in progress, cites Abbott in his bibliography. In 1963, *The Winter's Tale*, edited by J. H. P. Pafford, appeared; as early as line 27, Abbott is cited for elucidation: "For 'hath' as third person plural see Abbott, §334...."[37]

Abbott's conclusions concerning the relative merits of Elizabethan and modern English are contained in the conclusion to his Introduction:

> But for freedom, for brevity and for vigour, Elizabethan is superior to modern English. . . . We may perhaps claim some superiority in completeness and perspicuity for modern English, but if we were to appeal on this ground to the shade of Shakespeare in the words of Antonio in the *Tempest,*—
>
> "Do you hear us speak?"
> we might fairly be crushed with the reply of Sebastian—

---

[36] Abbott, p. 155.   [37] *Winter's Tale*, p. 4.

"I do; and surely
It is a sleepy language."[38]

If Abbott sometimes sounds pedantic, we should remember that he was writing as headmaster of the City of London School, and, indeed, the subtitle of his work is followed by the words "for the use of Schools."

"Simile and Metaphor," sections 516 through 529, are not, strictly speaking, part of Shakespeare grammar, and Abbott is no Coleridge defining fancy and imagination. What he attempts is to give five general rules concerning "Good and bad Metaphors." Like many critics, he is wary of Shakespeare's intense imagination. Abbott is disturbed by extraordinary imaginative fecundity which Matthew Arnold cautioned the young writer to beware. He too cautions restraint:

A metaphor must be wholly false, and must not combine truth with falsehood.

"A king is the pilot of the state," is a good metaphor. "A careful captain is the pilot of his ship," is a bad one. So
"Ere my tongue
Shall wound mine honour with such feeble wrong,
Or sound so base a parle,"—*Rich.* II. i. I. 190. is objectionable. The tongue, though it cannot "wound," can touch. It would have been better that "honour's" enemy should be intangible, that thereby the proportion and the perfection of the falsehood might be sustained. Honour can be wounded intangibly by "slander's venom'd spear" (*Rich.* II. i. I. 171); but, in a metaphor, not so well by the tangible tongue.[39]

Whatever reservations one has about a critic who analyzes metaphor this way, one cannot convict him of the overenthusiasm attributed to the Victorians at large. Brooks uses the breeches metaphor of Macbeth as an example of clothing imagery pervad-

[38] Abbott, p. 16.
[39] Abbott, p. 438.

ing the entire play. For this insight he is, as he acknowledges,[40] indebted to Caroline Spurgeon's *Shakespeare's Imagery and What It Tells Us*, first published in 1935. Miss Spurgeon's analysis of overriding imagery would have been much more difficult to accomplish in an era before Freud had explained how the unconscious succeeds in expressing itself despite seemingly successful repression. And Miss Spurgeon was anticipated by a Victorian clergyman whose work Abbott would have been in a unique position to exploit.

The Reverend Joshua Kirkman, M.A., contributed to the forty-eighth meeting of the New Shakspere Society (of which Abbott was a member) on Friday, January 10, 1879, a paper entitled "Animal Nature *versus* Human Nature in *King Lear*." What Kirkman does is catalogue the very high proportion of animal imagery running throughout *King Lear*.[41] If only some one had looked through *Macbeth* in search of some dominant imagery!

It is probably too much to claim that Abbott would have revised section 529 with a scholarly note on the relation between breeches and garments too vast for Macbeth, but Abbott was peculiarly suited to this kind of irregular and creative association. Like many Victorians, he was much more than appears to the casual critic. The article devoted to him in the *Dictionary of National Biography* cites his work of rebuilding the City of London School in terms that remind the modern reader of Thomas Arnold's work at Rugby. The article mentions his Broad Church sympathies and cites a number of his distinguished pupils, Sir Sidney Lee, Arthur Henry Bullen (the Elizabethan editor whose collections of old English plays came out in the 1880's), and Prime Minister Asquith. But the *D.N.B.* makes no mention of *Flatland: A Ro-*

---

[40] Brooks, p. 30.

[41] He in turn fails to acknowledge his indebtedness to the Reverend Walter Whiter, Clare College, Cambridge, a friend of Porson who published *A Specimen of a Commentary on Shakspeare Containing: I. Notes on As You Like It. II. An Attempt to Explain and Illustrate Various Passages, on a New Principle of Criticism Derived from Mr. Locke's Doctrine of the Association of Ideas.*

"People of the Period.—Poet Swinburne" (1870)

mance of Many Dimensions, published anonymously in the 1880's.[42] This is one of the earliest science-fiction satires, and is read today by people who know nothing of Abbott's scholarly activities. A recent edition is being sold alongside tales of interplanetary travel. What Abbott does here is combine the kind of social satire Butler employed in *Erewhon* with the progressive annihilation of time. And this seems to lie at the core of his theological writing as well. *From Letter to Spirit* attempts to eliminate the time gap separating Christ from the Victorians.[43] Abbott would have understood what G. Wilson Knight was to attempt half a century later, and Kirkman's technique combined with Abbott's insight might have opened whole vistas of productive scholarship. Both were Cambridge men too, Kirkman having been admitted pensioner at Queens in 1846 and Abbott at St. John's in 1857, and both seem to have lived in Hampstead at the same time without influencing each other.[44]

Kirkman's essay was more than a lucky shot. Somewhat earlier, Furnivall had stumbled onto the use of imagery as an aid in sorting out the confused authorship of *Henry VI*. Discussing a paper read at the twenty-seventh meeting of his New Shakspere Society, Friday, October 13, 1876, "On the Authorship of the Second and Third Parts of *Henry VI*, and their Originals," Furnivall noted:

> Critics seem to have made up their minds that only Greene, Marlowe, Peele, and Shakspere, had a hand in these plays. And yet there is one very markt feature in certain parts of *2 and 3 Henry VI*, which no reader can miss noticing, but which no critic has ever yet assignd to any of the authors he supposes to have been a joint writer of the plays. I allude to the many animal similes

---

[42] 2d rev. ed., London, 1884.

[43] London, 1903.

[44] I have supplemented the *D.N.B.* article on Abbott with the *Alumni Cantabrigienses, Part II from 1752–1900*, compiled by J. A. Venn, 6 vols. (Cambridge, 1940–54). Venn, in listing Abbott's publications, like the *D.N.B.*, omits his *Flatland*.

and metaphors. As Mr. Henry Stack puts it (with my enlargements) :—

"For metaphors, the play is a zoological garden, pasture and farmyard combined. Lions, curs[1], oxen[6] & [11], foxes[4] & [7], falcons[5] . . ."

Furnivall goes on tabulating for several lines, and then continues in his own racy prose:

Who then is this farmyard and menagerie man who often indulges in aphorisms? He is in *3 Henry VI* too. Is he one, or two or three? If he's Shakspere, if he's Greene, if he's Marlowe, or all of 'em, let him be recognizd, and parallel passages from him produced or referrd to. But I cannot consent to consider as final, any opinion on the authors of *2 and 3 Henry VI* which passes over in silence a star characteristic of this kind, and refuses to notice it when challengd so to do.[45]

Miss Jane Lee, author of the paper under discussion, was no Swinburne relishing the zest of check and assault. She responds rather primly:

Mr. Furnivall looks forward to the appearance of a critic who will be ready to take up the *Henry VI* Plays, and divide them scene by scene, and line by line, between the later and the earlier writers, saying: "Here Shakspere is reforming Greene"; "here is reforming Marlowe"; *etc.* In order to do this it will be necessary to say definitely who was the author of each separate scene and each separate line of the *Contention* and of the *True Tragedy.* When I wrote my paper on *Henry VI* some months ago I refused to do this, both because I felt some uncertainty as to whether or not Peele had any share in the old Plays; and, also, *because I felt (what, indeed, I still feel) that it is hazardous for any person with only the evidence of style to guide him to say positively that such particular words were written by such a particular writer.*[46]

[45] New Shakspere Society, *Transactions 1875–76*, pp. 280–83.
[46] New Shakespere Society, *Transactions 1875–76*, p. 289.

The problem of determining authorship is still with us, and my next chapter will explore it in detail. What has changed is the reliance on "style" to "positively" identify a writer. Scientific bibliographers try now for exactitude by examining the history of a text. This does not determine authorship so much as attempt to fix the identity of the word on the printed page, but not necessarily its meaning. Miss Lee seems to have been browbeaten by the energetic Furnivall, for she continued:

> If, however, it be thought by others that I am leaving my task unfinished, and it remains for some one else to undertake what I have not had the energy and the pluck to do, I feel bound to give up my own wishes in the matter, and to say to the best of my judgment what parts of the *Contention* and of the *True Tragedy* were most probably written by Marlowe, and what part by Greene.[47]

To the opening meeting of the New Shakspere Society held at University College on March 13, 1874, F. G. Fleay contributed a paper, read for him by Abbott, entitled "On Metrical Tests as Applied to Dramatic Poetry: Part I, Shakspere." At first, Fleay's work seemed a logical continuation of the direction Abbott had indicated. Fleay proposed to systematize quantitatively, whereas what Abbott attempted was essentially verbal, a logical systematization. A few lines are sufficient to indicate his early optimism concerning the scientific method: "Our analysis, which has hitherto been qualitative, must become quantitative; ... the test ... is this: Can you say, not only of what kind, but how much?"[48]

It is easy now to sneer at Fleay's solemnities, his applied Benthamism or Podsnappery. Almost from the first, contemporary critics expressed their reservations. The Variorum editor, himself

---

[47] New Shakspere Society, *Transactions 1875–76*, p. 289.

[48] New Shakspere Society, *Transactions 1874*, p. 2. Fleay attached great importance to this essay, and incorporated it into his *Shakespeare Manual* (London, 1876).

not averse to extracts and tabulation, said of the method: "No man on earth has done more of that kind of work than Fleay, and there's no second man on earth that accepts his conclusions—and when he comes to apply them to Shakespeare's plays, he scarcely accepts them himself in different editions of his own work."[49] Fleay wanted to fix precisely in time the moment Shakespeare wrote each of his plays by virtue of the verse tests he had devised. He seems to have been somewhat compulsive in his insistence on mathematical precision, and his subsequent career bears the mark of this neuroticism. But we cannot neglect his achievement if only because it now seems plain as day that Shakespeare used formal, closed, rhyming verse early in his career, gradually evolving toward the free style we associate with his final period. Even the very term "final period" was popularized by this strange, quarrelsome man whose career led him at last into the investigation of ancient Egyptian chronology.[50]

[49] *The Letters of Horace Howard Furness*, ed. H. H. F. J., I, 246. The first application of verse tests to Shakespeare seems to have been by Richard Roderick of Magdalen, Cambridge, who contributed to the sixth edition of Thomas Edwards' *Canons of Criticism*, an essay entitled "On the Metre of Henry VIII." Edwards is still lively reading, and deserves a paperback reprint. (In the copy I inspected at the New York Public Library, Roderick's contribution is untitled, and appears as the concluding section of his "Remarks on Shakespear" for *King Henry VIII* [pp. 225–28]).

[50] F. G. Fleay, *Egyptian Chronology: An Attempt to Conciliate the Ancient Schemes and to Educe a Rational System*. Dedicated to the memory of E. W. Benson, Lord Archbishop of Canterbury, and published by David Nutt, this essay, begun in 1892, attempts a chronology of the Egyptian dynasties along lines Fleay had used to date Shakespeare. He acknowledges the assistance of E. A. Abbott, who had also turned his attention backward in the direction of ancient chronology after completing his Shakespeare studies. Fleay anticipated the future of his researches with considerable optimism: "The present instalment is a portion of a larger work embracing the chronology of the Babylonians, Assyrians, Hebrews, &c., the appearance of which will depend on the sale of the present portion. Directly on the recoupment of the expense of its production the whole will be made ready for the press" (pp. xiii–xiv). Fleay lived until 1909, but no further installment was forthcoming. He died in Upper Tooting quite neglected by the world of letters.

To the introduction of his final study of Elizabethan literature, *A Biographical Chronicle of the English Drama 1559–1642*,[51] Fleay contributed a rambling recapitulation of his critical method. He repeats the brave credo of 1874, and quarrels with most of his colleagues from Halliwell to Collier with the notable exception of Swinburne, "to whom, by-the-bye, I owe a debt of gratitude for personally directing my attention to Chapman twenty-six years since."[52] But when he gets down to defending his method, Fleay expresses something we now take for granted. He deplores the mere accumulation of fact. The reader, he feels, is swamped beneath a mass of irrelevant and unrelated data. Today the complaint sounds modern, and his solution has for some time been a recognized principle of literary criticism. It is necessary, he says, to study an author by relating everything he wrote to each of his works and to the milieu that produced them. (This is the method Edmund Wilson employed so brilliantly in his investigation of Dickens.[53]) In the past twenty-five years, most literary studies have perforce analyzed an author's entire outlook in the course of evaluating his contribution. I quote a sentence from the all but last paragraph of Fleay's Introduction:

If the earlier literature of England has not lost for the coming generation all its interest through the detestable practice of cramming undeveloped brains with shilling primers and Clarendon Press editions with notes compiled from Concordances and Dictionaries (among which I do not include A. W. Ward's scholarly *Faustus and Friar Bacon*); if the study of dramatic history is to be continued in the future by any one outside a circle of faddists who think that in perpetual statement of individual opinion as to whether *Andronicus* is or is not good enough to be Shakespeare's

[51] 2 vols. (London, 1891).
[52] Fleay, *Biographical Chronicle*, I, 13.
[53] "Dickens: The Two Scrooges," in *Eight Essays* (New York, 1954). This essay was dedicated "To the Students of English 354, University of Chicago, Summer, 1939."

41

there can be any element of human interest; if the chronological succession of an author's works is a necessary basis for appreciating the value of each of them, and if the relations between different authors are of import in determining the position of each one in such a literary history, then such a book is absolutely necessary, not as being the history itself, but the preceding chronicle on which the history of a truly philosophical kind must necessarily be based.[54]

Fleay's metrical tests designed to place each play in time and space were fraught with flaws, and Furness was only one of many who recognized this. The same is true of his internal allusions, to which Chambers refers as "hasty generalizations and unstable hypotheses";[55] but Fleay's work served a more significant, though related function.

James Spedding (1808–81) contributed to the August, 1850, number of the *Gentleman's Magazine* the lead article, "Who Wrote Shakspere's Henry VIII?" After investigating internal differences of style, he concluded that most of the play was by Fletcher. Fleay's investigations of style took him much further. Halliday calls Fleay "the first of the disintegrators"[56] because his tests "proved" that a large part of what we attribute to Shakespeare was really the work of others. Halliday sides with Chambers, who wrote, "Modern essays at disintegrating the canon start from Fleay, whose own theories were ingenious if kaleidoscopic,

---

[54] Fleay, *Biographical Chronicle*, I, 14–15. E. K. Chambers pays his respects to Fleay in the List of Authorities cited in the first volume of *The Elizabethan Stage*: "Some new ground was broken by F. G. Fleay, who gave real stimulus to investigation by the series of hasty generalizations and unstable hypotheses contained in his *On the Actor Lists, 1578–1642* (R. H. Soc. Trans. ix. 44), *On the History of Theatres in London, 1576–1642* (R. H. Soc. Trans. x. 114), *Shakespeare Manual* (1876, 1878), *Introduction to Shakespearian Study* (1877), *Life and Work of Shakespeare* (1886), *Chronicle History of the London Stage* (1890), and *Biographical Chronicle of the English Drama* (1891)." I, xv–xvi.

[55] *The Elizabethan Stage*, I, xv.

[56] F. E. Halliday, *A Shakespeare Companion 1550–1950*, p. 207.

but who called attention to many features of the texts, both stylistic and bibliographical, which are still receiving study."[57]

But, as Johnson might have suspected, neither Fleay nor Spedding was making wholly original contributions. Spedding's August contribution to the *Gentleman's Magazine* had been signed "J. S." In October, he identified himself in an article again entitled "Who Wrote Shakspere's Henry VIII?" beginning: "I was much gratified, though not at all surprised, to find, by a letter from Mr. Samuel Hickson to the editor of 'Notes and Queries,' (No. 43, p. 198), that the question 'Who Wrote Henry VIII?' had already engaged that gentleman's attention, and that he had come to the same conclusion with myself as to the parts that were written by Fletcher."[58]

Hickson based his claim for priority on a long article he had contributed to the April, 1847, issue of the *Westminster and Foreign Quarterly Review*, entitled "The Two Noble Kinsmen."[59] This was a review of three works concerning Beaumont and Fletcher, but it was devoted principally to a determination, on the basis of style, of the parts by Shakespeare. The most interesting work reviewed was an anonymous volume published in Edinburgh in 1833 entitled *A Letter on Shakspere's Authorship of The Two Noble Kinsmen*. Hickson knew that the author was William Spalding, and he acknowledged the appropriateness of verse study in determining the authorship of any disputed play. Spalding died in 1859, but after his death the verse test was liberally used by members of the New Shakspere Society to date all Shakespeare's work. In 1876, Furnivall, founder of the New Shakspere Society, reprinted Spalding's letter along with Spedding's article from the August, 1850, *Gentleman's Magazine*.

Naturally, verse tests are subject to all the permutations inherent

---

[57] Chambers, *William Shakespeare*, I, 208.

[58] *Gentleman's Magazine*, October, 1850, p. 381.

[59] Pages 59–88.

in arithmetic order, and Fleay was only the most conspicuous and persistent expander of Spalding's theory. Roderick had merely observed the phenomenon, without developing a theory: "What Shakespear intended by all this, I fairly own myself ignorant."[60]

Two years later, a member of the New Shakspere Society suggested still another permutation. Frederick S. Pulling began his address on November 14, 1879, with the following paragraph:

> Professor Dowden in his admirable little "Shakspere Primer," after enumerating the different tests which have been applied, with such interesting results, to determine the chronology of Shakspere's plays, mentions that two other solvents have been suggested and described; one of which is the "speech-ending test" of Professor Ingram. This test had only been partially worked out by its inventor, but it appeared to me that it would be highly desirable that it should be thoroughly investigated, for the purpose of discovering whether it would not supply additional evidence to enable us to decide on the much-vexed question of the exact chronology of the Plays—especially of those of the middle period.[61]

None of the men I have cited is a "traditional" Victorian critic, and not one of them indulged in what we have been led to believe is the traditional Victorian confusion between art and morality. Abbott ventures no opinion whatever concerning Shakespeare's private life. He is scrupulously detached as the most demanding

[60] Edwards, *Canons of Criticism*, p. 228.

[61] New Shakspere Society, *Transactions 1877–79*, p. 457. The variations are truly endless, and some idea of how much research has gone into this kind of investigation can be had by glancing at the bibliographical notes to Chapter VII, "The Problem of Authenticity," and Chapter VIII, "The Problem of Chronology," in volume I of E. K. Chambers' *William Shakespeare*, and Appendix H, Metrical Tables, Vol. II, pp. 397–408. This cutting Shakespeare down to size reflects the antiheroic tendency of Victorian literature, and we will return to it when discussing hero-worship in the next chapter. As an example of machine technology with its interchangeability of parts, it is characteristically nineteenth century.

New Critic at Downing College; indeed, his method is necessarily a model of impartiality and, as such, should have commended itself to the early-twentieth-century critics. Fleay himself says surprisingly little about the man for all his subsequent notoriety or the absurdity to which he drove his method.[62] Halliwell-Phillipps, the only one of our critics whose work covers the span of both Shakespeare societies, may be quoted for his considered opinion. Writing (in 1882, at the culmination of his career) the Preface to his *Outlines of the Life of Shakespeare*,[63] a title by the way suggestive in its modesty of Chambers' *William Shakespeare: A Study of Facts and Problems*, Halliwell-Phillipps expresses his mature judgment:

> In the absence of some very important discovery, the general and intense desire to penetrate the mystery which surrounds the personal history of Shakespeare cannot be wholly gratified. Something, however, may be accomplished in that direction by a diligent and critical study of the materials now accessible, especially if care be taken to avoid the temptation of endeavouring to decipher his inner life and character through the media of his works. . . . It will dissipate many an illusion, amongst others the propriety of criticism being grounded upon a reverential belief in the unvarying perfection of Shakespeare's dramatic art. He, indeed, unquestionably obtained a complete mastery over that art at an early period of his literary career, but his control over it was continually liable to be governed by the customs and exigencies of

[62] Fleay's article, "On the Motive of Shakspere's Sonnets," *Macmillan's Magazine* (May, 1875), 433–45, seems designed to counteract the growing innuendo of homosexuality and general promiscuity which became more prominent in the Edwardian era.

[63] J. O. Halliwell-Phillipps, *Outlines of the Life of Shakespeare*. Halliwell became Halliwell-Phillipps in 1872 upon the death of his wife's father, the famous collector by whom he had been occasionally employed as literary agent of sorts and who never forgave the match. For a full account of Sir Thomas Phillipps' tangled life and a correction of Sidney Lee's *D.N.B.* piece on Halliwell, see A.N.L. Munby, *The Family Affairs of Sir Thomas Phillipps, Phillipps Studies No. 2* (Cambridge, 1952), and the general index to Vols. 1–5 in *The Dispersal of the Phillipps Library, Phillipps Studies No. 5* (Cambridge, 1960).

the ancient stage, so much so that, in not a few instances, the action of a scene was diverted for the express purpose of complying with those necessities. It should be remembered that his dramas were not written for posterity, but as a matter of business, never for his own speculations but always for that of the managers of his own day, the choice of subject being occasionally dictated by them or by patrons of the stage. . . . Neither does it appear at all probable that he could have had time, under the conditions in which he worked, for the studied application of those subtle devices underlying his art which are attributed to his sagacity by the philosophical critics, and some of which, it is amusing to notice, may be equally observed, if they exist at all, in the original plot-sources of his dramas. . . . The phenomenon of a moral unity is not to be found either in nature or in the works of nature's poet, whose truthful and impartial genius could never have voluntarily endured a submission to a preconception which involved violent deviations from the course prescribed by his sovereign knowledge of human nature and the human mind.[64]

This is, admittedly, a long paragraph, from which I have given only extracts, but it is worth quoting for the flavor of Victorian criticism, more leisurely than the analysis via historical perspective we are accustomed to today. Yet, for all the wordiness of those seeming unhurried times, it is free from the gush or adulation our own century has been in the habit of projecting back onto the nineteenth. Restraint and critical austerity seem to characterize the paragraph, and I wonder how much of it the typical *Scrutiny* subscriber, subjected to one of I. A. Richards' poetry quizzes, would have to read before identifying it as late Victorian. Possibly the style gives it away, although the restraint and content might confuse one of Leavis' disciples. Indeed, there is something Coleridgean and also modern in the notion of emasculating a text from its cultural content and analyzing it in antiseptic isolation.

In any passionate argument, one inevitably runs the risk of

[64] Halliwell-Phillipps, *Outlines of the Life of Shakespeare*, pp. vi–x.

selecting material that bolsters the argument to the exclusion of contrary evidence. Something of this sort is inevitable, given the inherent fallibility of an investigator, but I have begun with Collier, whose history was published in 1831, five years before *Pickwick Papers* and nearly a decade before the Carlyle selections with which Nichol Smith concludes his survey of romantic criticism. Halliwell-Phillipps began publishing in the late 1830's, was at the age of twenty a founder of Collier's first Shakespeare Society in 1840, and died in 1889,[65] the same year as Browning and Gerard Manley Hopkins. Surely, the Victorian period was ending. Cardinal Newman and Richard William Church died the next year. Rimbaud, Renan, Tennyson, and Richard Owen were all dead by 1892. It seems, looking over these fifty years in retrospect, that a scientific habit and a theory of methodology applied to Shakespearean studies were, together, one characteristic of the Victorian age.

Nor is this the imposed judgment of hindsight applied half a century after the event. Summing up the contribution of Victorian scholarship for the second edition of his three-volume *History of English Dramatic Literature* (1899), the year Noel Coward was born, when by any account the age had ended, A. W. Ward says very much the same thing:

> Another lettered generation was however growing up in this country, which for the most part, in so far as it directed its energies to the study and elucidation of the greatest of English writers, preferred to occupy itself primarily with the material part of his works. Herein they not only followed traditions handed down by such commentators as Steevens and Malone, and continued by Drake in his elaborate tomes, but showed themselves awake to the demands made upon students of Shakspere by the new era that had opened in the European world of letters for historical and philological criticism. . . . English Shakspere-study has during the

[65] Hitler's birth that year is another convenient emblem of the age to come.

greater part of the present century been chiefly concerned with the elucidation and restoration of his text, the explanation and illustration of his matter, and the history of all that entered into or surrounded his life and literary career.[66]

To establish Ward's credentials, let me note that he is the first authority on the history of Elizabethan drama acknowledged by E. K. Chambers in the Introduction to his *Elizabethan Stage*.[67] He is also the same Ward whom Fleay honorably excluded from complicity in "the detestable practice of cramming undeveloped brains with shilling primers and Clarendon Press editions."[68] A man who can keep the respect of his most quarrelsome contemporary while retaining the next generation's admiration may safely be relied on. But the notion of a Victorian scholarly method dies hard. Contributing a signed article to a special number of the *Times Literary Supplement* called "The Critical Moment," Harry Levin digresses momentarily with a paragraph on recent Shakespeare scholarship:

> As we draw near to Shakespeare's 400th anniversary, I am convinced that he stands nearer to us than he did to his readers and spectators during most of the intervening years. That proximity is partly due to a renewed concentration on him in his natural habitat, the theatre, and partly on the accumulation of studies casting light on his original texts, his rhetorical means, his antiquarian

[66] Adolphus William Ward, *A History of English Dramatic Literature to the Death of Queen Anne*, I, 569.

[67] Chambers, p. xvii.

[68] Fleay, *Biographical Chronicle*, I, 15. Ward was more cautious in evaluating Fleay: "Of Mr. F. G. Fleay's *Chronicle History of the London Stage, 1559–1642* . . . as of companion books by the same author, time may be trusted to digest some of the conclusions, without in any way impairing the credit due to a single-minded candour and indefatigable research." (Ward I, 1 n.) He was more generous to Fleay's "method of inquiry" in the obituary he contributed to the *Athenaeum*, March 27, 1909, pp. 375–76. Both Ward and his wife were grandchildren of Thomas Arnold's sister and therefore in the mainstream of Victorian intellectual life.

background, and his intellectual climate. Scholars of E. K. Chambers's generation spent industrious and productive careers in gaining public access to the facts, the documents, and the other relevant materials, so that the next generation—not without gratitude—could undertake to synthesize and interpret with more freedom and more security.[69]

Chambers died in 1954. His first important work, *The Medieval Stage*, appeared in 1903, a year that saw Conrad's *Typhoon*, James's *Ambassadors*, Shaw's *Man and Superman*, and Edward VII seated very securely on the throne.

Dr. Johnson is credited with the observation that we tend to judge living authors by their worst work and the dead by their best. A similar split seems to have been operating in the world of scholarship. If Victorian critics developed scientific procedure along with a concern for moral conviction, we have tended to appropriate the former to our own century while stigmatizing their excess of the latter.

But those moralists whom everyone associates with an over-earnest Victorian milieu—those misguided men confusing art with morality whom the twentieth century was to set straight in so many ways—where are they: Dowden, Furnivall, and Swinburne? They will be considered in my next chapter.

[69] *Times Literary Supplement*, July 26, 1963, p. 565.

OF ALL OUR STUDY the last end and aim should be to ascertain how a great writer or artist has served the life of man; to ascertain this, to bring home to ourselves as large a portion as may be the gain wherewith he has enriched human life, and to render access to that store of wisdom, passion, and power, easier and surer for others.

—Edward Dowden, "The Interpretation of Literature," *Transcripts and Studies* (1896)

The plays of Shakespeare's later years which Renan admired so much breathe another spirit.

—The spirit of reconciliation, the quaker librarian breathed.

—There can be no reconciliation, Stephen said, if there has not been a sundering. . . .

—He died dead drunk, Buck Mulligan capped. A quart of ale is a dish for a king. O, I must tell you what Dowden said!

—What? asked Besteglinton.

William Shakespeare and company, limited. The people's William. For terms apply: E. Dowden, Highfield house. . . .

—Lovely! Buck Mulligan suspired amorously. I asked him what he thought of the charge of pederasty brought against the bard. He lifted his hands and said: *All we can say is that life ran very high in those days.* Lovely!

Catamite.

—James Joyce, *Ulysses*

the moral victorians

Stately plump Buck Mulligan is paraphrasing the first sentence of Dowden's *Shakspere*, a volume in J. R. Green's series of literature primers for schoolchildren. Dowden begins: "In the closing years of the sixteenth century the life of England ran high," and it is appropriate that Joyce cites a text for schoolchildren (rather than one of Dowden's many works for an adult audience) in order to discredit a Dublin intellectual of the preceding generation. Of course Lytton Strachey, another Bloomsbury darling, was working the same vein when he associated Thomas Arnold's shortness of breath with Rugby's high moral aspiration.

What Joyce does in the section on Shakespeare is divert or invert the preoccupation of Victorian critics while retaining the methodology constructed by them. The themes Stephen elaborates were suggested in the nineteenth century, and—more important—the comparative method he employed had been devised by men of the preceding generation. Only the emphasis differs. Most Victorians, when they came to interpret, tended to regularize Shakespeare's sexual conduct, whereas Stephen shocks by boldly flaunting his emancipation from the canon of repression that governed his lower-middle-class Dublin milieu.

Even this suggested pederasty was far from an original contribution. Charles Kingsley, who died in 1875, thought of Shakespeare as unmanly: "And in what that same strength consists, not even the dramatic imagination of a Shakespeare could discover.

What are those heart-rending sonnets of his, but the confession that over and above all his powers he lacked one thing, and knew not what it was, or where to find it—and that was—to be strong?"[1] It was common coin in the 1880's, when Walter Pater's *Appreciations* appeared with the new essay "Shakespeare's English Kings," analyzing Richard II in terms of his femininity.[2] Butler's *Shakespeare's Sonnets Reconsidered* and Oscar Wilde's *Portrait of Mr. W. H.* belong to the 1890's. Frank Harris had planned to call *The Women of Shakespeare*[3] "The Woman Shakespeare,"[4] although he explicitly denies the implication of pederasty. Since Harris, at least by his own account, seems to have pulled out all the stops in the course of a tumultuous existence, his opinion seems worth recording.[5]

The habit of relating Shakespeare's works to one another was at the heart of Fleay's method, and the close search for incidents outside the plays that would throw light on them was another point on which he insisted, too stridently perhaps. "There can be no reconciliation, Stephen said, if there has not been a sundering." In the sense that the sundering and reconciliation may be traced through a series of plays rather than one, Joyce owes a debt to two sets of Victorian criteria: first, that which imposed a scientific (by which I mean an essentially quantitative) order on each of the

---

[1] "The Limits of Exact Science as Applied to History," in *The Roman and the Teuton* (London, 1891), p. 331.

[2] London, 1889.

[3] London, 1911.

[4] Page ix.

[5] Eric Partridge, in *Shakespeare's Bawdy* (New York, 1948), corroborates my suggestion that the homosexual Shakespeare is an Edwardian development, although he does not exonerate Frank Harris. "The charge was first brought in 1889 by a homosexual (Oscar Wilde). . . . But as Oscar Wilde, though his *Portrait* provided excellent reading, egregiously failed to substantiate his charge; so too did Samuel Butler, in 1899, with *Shakespeare's Sonnets*, where the 'evidence' is childish; so too Frank Harris, in 1909, with *The Man Shakespeare*, where he dragged the dramatist down to his own level." (Pages 13, 14.)

F. J. Furnivall in 1901

plays; and next, on what is essentially a second set which interpreted or enriched this order by imposing qualitative judgments
onto the preceding quantitative measurement.[6] Most of this research is polarized around the New Shakspere Society, which attempted unsuccessfully to mesh both sets of criteria. The society's
founder, Frederick James Furnivall, explained that its purpose
was to arrange Shakespeare's life into periods, and the language
he used suggests that the reason was to derive a moral purpose out
of the mass of statistical information the age was then accumulat-
ing. Like all logicians, Furnivall defines the object to be sought in
his original prospectus:

> The purpose of our Society . . . is, by a very close study of the
> metrical and phraseological peculiarities of Shakspere, to get his
> plays as nearly as possible into the order in which he wrote them;
> to check that order by the higher tests of imaginative power,
> knowledge of life, self-restraint in expression, weight of thought,
> depth of purpose; and then to use that revised order for the purpose
> of studying the progress and meaning of Shakspere's mind, the
> passage of it from the fun and word-play, the lightness, the pas-
> sion, of the Comedies of Youth, through the patriotism (still with
> comedy of more meaning) of the Histories of Middle Age, to the
> great Tragedies dealing with the deepest questions of man in

[6] G. M. Young has nothing at all to say about Shakespeare in his *Victorian
England* (first published in 1936), but he observes, broadly speaking, that early
Victorians were dominated by measurement whereas the late Victorian mind
imposed interpretation on the mass of fact already gathered: "We are passing
from the statistical to the historical age, where the ground and explanation of
ideas, as of institutions, is looked for in their origins: their future calculated by
observation of the historic curve. As Early Victorian thought is regulated by the
conception of progress, so the late Victorian mind is overshadowed by the doctrine of evolution. But the idea of progress—achieved by experiment, consolidated
by law or custom, registered by statistics—had, without much straining of logic
or conscience, been made to engage with the dominant Protestant faith, and this,
equally, in both its modes: in the individualism of the soul working out its own
salvation, in the charity which sought above all things the welfare of others."
(Page 163.)

Later Life; and then at last to the poet's peaceful and quiet home-
life again in Stratford . . . .[7]

Furnivall is addicted to long sentences, and this one goes on for
several lines more. But the quotation is long enough to indicate
where Stephen derived the insight that made all Dublin gasp for
admiration. And if we look backward to Rowe's Preface of 1709,
in which he suggests that Shakespeare's best plays may be the work
of his earliest youth because "they were the most vigorous, and
had the most fire and strength of Imagination in 'em. . . ."[8] we can
approximate the time when modern scientific habit takes root.
Furnivall lamented that no one in England had dealt with Shakespeare as a whole: "It is a disgrace to England . . . that no book by
an Englishman exists which deals in any worthy manner with
Shakspere as a whole."[9] G. G. Gervinus, as early as 1850, had
divided Shakespeare into three periods. His *Shakespeare Commen-*
taries was translated into English in 1863, and Furnivall wrote a
preface to the English translation in 1877.

In retrospect, Victorians were well aware of this achievement.
It represents the only worthwhile idea in Leslie Stephen's "Shakespeare as a Man":

Minute students of Shakespeare have done one great service at
least. They have established approximately the order of his works.
. . . We watch Shakespeare from the start; beginning as a cobbler
and adapter of other men's works; making a fresh start as a fol-
lower of Marlowe, and then improving upon his model in the
great historical dramas. . . . If some knowledge of Shakespeare is
implied in a comparison between him and his contemporaries,

[7] New Shakspere Society, *Transactions, 1874*, p. vi.
[8] Rowe, I, vii.
[9] *The Succession of Shakspere's Works: Being the Introduction to Professor
Gervinus's "Commentaries on Shakespeare,"* p. xix. Furnivall had this essay published as a separate pamphlet in the fall of 1874. Note the contention of Gervinus
that "the man who first valued Shakespeare according to his full desert was in-
disputably Lessing." G. G. Gervinus, *Shakespeare Commentaries,* p. 13.

54

there is still more significance in the comparison with himself. A century ago a critic [Coleridge?] put the *Two Gentlemen of Verona* at the end and the *Winter's Tale* at the beginning of his career. Such an inversion, we now perceive, would make the whole history of his mental development chaotic and contradictory.[10]

The first of the interpretive criticisms in English, and still the most famous,[11] Dowden's *Shakespere: A Critical Study of His Mind and Art*,[12] appeared in 1875. Dowden seems to have been working toward a key to the organization of Shakespeare independent of Furnivall and the New Shakspere Society. This parallel effort tends to confirm that his habit of mind, organizing Shakespeare into distinct periods comparable to laws of natural evolution, was a characteristic of the age. Dowden, teaching at Trinity College, Dublin, sought the same kind of explanation as other scholars across the sea in London. In a letter to Aubrey de Vere, dated August 22, 1874 (the year Furnivall's New Shakspere Society got under way), Dowden confides: "My Shakespeare[13] lectures get on very slowly; but they will in the end get written. . . . If you have anything to say, or have heard Sir Henry Taylor say anything, on this subject, I should be rejoiced to get a letter from you: *How is the personality of a dramatic poet to be discovered.*"[14] Dowden's emphasis is on the adjective "dramatic," and it is dramatic personality that interests Dowden, as it had Keats some fifty years before. Dowden is an appropriate biographer for Wordsworth and Shelley. His search for purpose, inner law, and the dramatic secret

[10] *National Review*, XXXVII (1901), 229–30. Reprinted in *Studies of a Biographer*, IV, 23–24.

[11] A 1962 copy (p. iv) informs the reader that this is the twenty-fifth impression (of the third edition).

[12] London.

[13] Later in life, Dowden reverted to the traditional spelling and apparently edited his correspondence accordingly; at the time, his published writings conform to the spelling "Shakspere." Coleridge had reversed the procedure, switching from "Shakespeare" to "Shakspeare" about the time his lectures began.

[14] *Letters of Edward Dowden and His Correspondents*, p. 69.

is an inheritance of that romanticism to the recording of which he devoted so much energy.

Furnivall consistently sought these qualities in German scholarship. He had declared that no "Englishman had dealt in any worthy manner with Shakespeare as a whole," and had concluded the first paragraph of his Introduction to the *Commentaries* with: "The profound and generous 'Commentaries' of Gervinus—an honour to a German to have written, a pleasure to an Englishman to read—is still the only book known to me that comes near the true treatment and the dignity of its subject, or can be put into the hands of the student who wants to know the mind of Shakspere."[15] Thus the palm is awarded German scholarship. But independent of Gervinus, Charles Knight, that publisher of a "popular type" to whom A. W. Ward referred in his *History of English Dramatic Literature* . . .,[16] seems to have thought this out for himself. Like Gervinus, he opted for three periods. I quote from his autobiography, *Passages from the Life of Charles Knight*:

> As I advanced in my Shaksperian studies, [Knight reverting to eighteenth-century practice, anticipated Furnivall's spelling] I found that my labours would not cease with the acquirement of a more intimate knowledge of all that had been written about the text, but that I must carefully examine the various opinions as to the order in which the plays of Shakspere were produced, unless I were implicitly to adopt the theories advocated in Malone's "Essay" on that very difficult subject. I was satisfied that much depended in coming to something like accurate conclusions as to the plays which belong respectively to the poet's earlier period, his middle period, and his later period. The historical plays would necessarily follow in the order of the events of which they were the subject. But for the comedies and tragedies, I determined to print them in the order which I believed to be at least an approximation to the period of their composition.[17]

[15] G. G. Gervinus, *Shakespeare Commentaries*, p. xxi.
[16] I, 569.

Knight is reminiscing over his labors in the year 1837; hence some allowance should be made for his conclusion, although the procedure is sound.

It was also Knight who defended the Shakespearian integrity of the three parts of *Henry VI* nearly a century before this became fashionable. His arguments are imbedded in the rambling "An Essay on the Three Parts of King Henry VI, and King Richard III" in the *Pictorial Edition of the Works of Shakspere.*[18]

In addition, this essay anticipates two further but related advances in scholarship. In 1929, Peter Alexander published *Shakespeare's Henry VI and Richard III* (Cambridge), in which he demonstrated that *The First Part of the Contention* (1594) and *The True Tragedy of Richard Duke of York* (1595) are corrupt versions of the second and third parts of *Henry VI.* This absolved Shakespeare from having begun his apprenticeship by cribbing from other authors unnamed, since *The First Part of the Contention* as well as *The True Tragedy* are really Shakespeare's work. (Alexander suggests that the actor who played Suffolk and Cade in *The First Part of the Contention* and Warwick and Clifford in *The True Tragedy* attempted to reconstruct the entire play.)

Although Knight does not specify how the text became so bad beyond his surmise that these plays are early sketches, he reaches the same conclusion concerning Shakespeare's hand in them: ". . . the 'First Part of the Contention,' and the 'Richard Duke of York' (more commonly called 'The Second Part of the Contention') being in fact Shakspere's own work, in an imperfect state."[19]

In 1951, F. P. Wilson delivered the Clark Lectures. His title was *Marlowe and the Early Shakespeare*[20] and the final lecture was devoted to the early historical plays concerning Shakespeare's

[17] Charles Knight, *Passages from the Life of Charles Knight*, p. 386.

[18] Knight, *Pictorial Edition of the Works of Shakspere*, V, 401–82 (Histories, Vol. II).

[19] Knight, *Pictorial . . . Shakspere*, V, 404 (Histories II, 404).

[20] Oxford, 1953.

debt to earlier practitioners of the genre: "My conclusion is, though I am frightened at my own temerity in saying so, that for all we know there were no popular plays on English history before the Armada and that Shakespeare may have been the first to write one."[21] Knight too, around 1840, argued for originality in the face of scholarly opposition, principally Malone's. The most interesting part of his essay sets out to prove "not who first wrote historical plays, but who first wrote historical plays in the spirit of an artist. . . . We will now ask, what other historical plays of any poetical pretension were in existence in 1589?"[22]

To this point, we have been tracing the actual contribution of Victorians to Shakespeare scholarship, with a minimum of interpolation. But in order to understand these "interpreters" against whom most criticism of Victorian Shakespeare studies was directed, some digression is necessary.

Writers of the earlier twentieth century were quite right to observe that, by and large, these men superimposed a purpose on the dramatic text which may not have been there. We are all familiar with the excesses of this method and the numerous examples pointed out to us of interpretation on which no two critics see eye to eye. The selections W. W. Lawrence collected on *Measure for Measure* are a fair example.[23] The enormous diversity of inter-

[21] Wilson, p. 108.

[22] Knight, *Pictorial* . . . *Shakspere*, V, 442 (Histories, II, 442). In 1964, Peter Alexander told me that in the 1920's excessive reliance on the research of E. K. Chambers allowed younger men to overlook Knight's essay although Knight had, along with Dyce and the young James Halliwell, been a founder of the original Shakespeare Society (1840). Chambers' unfamiliarity with Knight is further suggested by Knight's absence from the list of authorities cited by Chambers in his essay "Edward the Third" (*William Shakespeare*, I, 515–18). Knight, in 1838, anticipated Swinburne's argument of the 1870's that Shakespeare had no part in the play, and Swinburne acknowledges Knight (Algernon Charles Swinburne, *A Study of Shakespeare*, pp. 270–71).

[23] Lawrence, *Shakespeare's Problem Comedies*, Chap. 3. Gervinus felt that Desdemona was punished for having disobeyed her father, a concept particularly

pretation brought to the plays, along with the general charge that the Victorians had nothing in particular to say, comprised the tenor of early twentieth-century criticism. Now I shall digress to say something about the environment that surrounded moral interpretation and its attribution to Shakespeare.

The leisurely paragraph in Halliwell-Phillipps' introduction (quoted near the end of the preceding chapter) should not be taken to represent the Victorian tenor of life. Halliwell-Phillipps was writing (1882) near the close of his life, in prosperity and the retirement of Hollingbury Copse, Brighton. The language and easy expansiveness confirm a general impression that Victorian times were leisurely and populated by confident men with a secure sense of their own importance. Contemporary evidence suggests that the truth was different, and Shakespeare criticism reflects in part the needs of society.

William Rathbone Greg, Walter Bagehot's brother-in-law and W. W. Greg's father, was a prolific essayist through most of the Victorian period. The elder Greg's opinion is worth citing because he represents the spirit of independent capitalism that flourished most brightly around mid-century.[24] There are some echoes of Gradgrind and whiffs of Pecksniff in his work, but that only suggests the relevance of Dickens to any interpretation of the mid-Victorian milieu.

In April, 1851, Greg contributed to the *Edinburgh Review*[25] a

congenial to Victorian sensibilities. But "the poet, by this conclusion, has not once for all condemned *every* unequal marriage, nor *every* secret union, just as little as in Romeo he has condemned all passionate love" (*Shakespeare Commentaries*, p. 546).

[24] Bagehot and Greg married the first and second daughters, respectively, of James Wilson, founder of the *Economist*. W(alter) W(ilson) Greg, named for his famous uncle, in his youth was being groomed as editor of that family-owned enterprise until he settled on literary studies. Curiously, both Wilson and Greg were unsuccessful businessmen who later regained financial independence defending free enterprise, under which they themselves had failed.

[25] Pages 305–39.

long article entitled "England as It Is," principally a rebuttal of the severe judgment passed on society by one William Johnston in *England as It Is, Political, Social, and Industrial, in the Middle of the Nineteenth Century.*[26] Greg argues that things are really much better than Johnston alleges, that they are improving in most places most of the time, and that certain privations are the responsibility of the lower classes themselves. I quote, therefore, Greg's description of England as it is:

> The excessive toil required in nearly every occupation—the severity of the struggle for existence—the strain upon the powers of every man who runs the race of life in this land and age of high excitement,—Mr Johnston regards as a great counter-indication to the idea of progress. Unquestionably it is a great drawback, and a sore evil. But it is by no means confined to the lower orders. Throughout the whole community we are all called to labour too early and compelled to labour too severely and too long. We live sadly too fast. Our existence, in nearly all ranks, is a crush, a struggle, and a strife. Immensely as the field of lucrative employment has been enlarged, it is still too limited for the numbers that crowd into it. The evil is not peculiar to the peasant or the handicraftsman—perhaps even it is not most severely felt by him. The lawyer, the statesman, the student, the artist, the merchant, all groan under the pressure. All who work at all are overworked. Some have more to do than they can do without sacrificing the enjoyments, the amenities, and all the higher objects of existence; others can scarcely find work enough to enable them to keep body and soul together. No one can be more keenly alive than we are to all that is regrettable in such a state of things.[27]

It is appropriate that 1859 should boast the first edition of Samuel Smiles' *Self-Help.* An age when society could offer the individual so little assistance inevitably drove him inward searching for aid.

[26] London, 1851.
[27] W. R. Greg, *Edinburgh Review*, April, 1851, pp. 324–25, collected in *Miscellaneous Essays*, pp. 169–70.

But these conditions did not produce the hero or even his caricature associated with Mr. Barrett of Wimpole Street. George Eliot's novels are the handiest illustration of these two ideas. To depict leisurely time, she is forced backward toward the dawn of the nineteenth century, very often contrasting the rapidity of modern life with England as it was. This, from *Adam Bede*, is representative:

> Old Leisure . . . was a contemplative, rather stout gentleman, of excellent digestion,—of quiet perceptions, undiseased by hypothesis: happy in his inability to know the causes of things, preferring the things themselves. . . .
>
> Fine old Leisure! Do not be severe upon him, and judge him by our modern standards; he never went to Exeter Hall, or heard a popular preacher, or read "Tracts for the Times" of "Sartor Resartus."[28]

Of course her *Middlemarch* is concerned principally with the inability to live according to a heroic ideal in the nineteenth century: "Many Theresas have been born who found for themselves no epic life wherein there was a constant unfolding of far-resonant action; . . . for these later-born Theresas were helped by no coherent social faith and order which could perform the function of knowledge for the ardently willing soul."[29] For George Eliot, the trinity of God, immortality, and duty had been reduced to stern Unitarian duty. Higher criticism of the Bible and Darwin's *Origin of Species* enforced the concept of law and necessity. These made it increasingly difficult for educated men to believe in a divine saviour or even in a contemporary hero, since he too would be bound in fetters of necessity. I think these ideas were strengthened by the concepts of the Manchester economists then in ascendency, men who could argue for the necessity of economic privation on the grounds that nature's law sanctioned free competition and that any interference was a violation of natural law.

[28] *Adam Bede*, Chap. 52.
[29] *Middlemarch*, Prelude, paragraph 2.

One reaction to the growing dehumanization of the universe was hero-worship. The Victorians gave up ground grudgingly and attempted to transfer sublime or near-divine attributes from a personal God to men of near godlike perfections. Walter E. Houghton divides his book *The Victorian Frame of Mind 1830– 1870* into fourteen chapters, of which Chapter 12 is called "Hero-Worship." He finds that heroes began assuming the attributes of God rather late in the Victorian period. This fits in with the timing of interpretive Shakespeare criticism; Dowden's *Shakspere: A Critical Study of His Mind and Art* was published in 1875, and the New Shakspere Society, around which most of this interpretive criticism clustered, came to an end in 1894.

> It is quite right, I think, to see a connection between, on the one hand, finding a substitute for religion, and on the other, the heaven-born character of Scott's *Waverley* and George Sand's *Indiana*—as well as the *Iliad* and *Odyssey*. . . . when God was dead, the gods and heroes of history or of myth could take his place and save the moral sum of things. What Mary Sibree said of herself—that under George Eliot's influence her interest shifted from Christianity "towards manifestations of nobility," like that of the Marquis von Posa in *Don Carlos*, who roused in her "an enthusiasm for heroism and virtue"—was true, I think, of many Victorians, *especially late Victorians*.[30] [My italics.]

Houghton does not describe Shakespeare in these terms. Indeed, he tends to emphasize the Victorian undercurrent of reservation toward Shakespeare's sexuality.[31] But further in the same para-

[30] Houghton, *The Victorian Frame of Mind 1830–1870*, pp. 321–22.

[31] Contrary to the meaning of the verb derived from his name, Thomas Bowdler did not consider his text an "improvement." Bowdler approached Shakespeare's written word with great reverence and proceeded to delete what he thought hurtful or inappropriate only because he knew complete "unbowdlerized" texts would survive alongside his own. I quote from the Preface to his first edition: "If a presumptuous artist should undertake to remove a supposed defect in the Transfiguration of Raphael, or in the Belvidere Apollo, and in making the attempt should injure one of those invaluable productions of art and

graph he quotes Frederic Harrison's *Autobiographic Memoirs* and the devotions undertaken by English Comtists: "One of the most popular forms of commemoration which we instituted was that of a pilgrimage to the home, or tomb, and associations of great men, and visits to scenes of historic interest. The most elaborate of these were visits to Stratford-on-Avon and its neighbourhood, to Oxford, Cambridge, and Huntington, to Paris, Winchester, and Canterbury. . . ."[32]

The hero in eclipse has become a commonplace of Victorian criticism. Carlyle, Kingsley, and Ruskin might plead for a contemporary hero, but their own inspiration was invariably drawn from the past. The very urgency and intensity of their appeal suggest that among their contemporaries the heroic model was lacking. It is only among the relatively well-satisfied entrepreneurial class that one comes across the fatalistic suggestion that each generation selects its heroes from the preceding ages, preferably a generation whose outlines are already receding toward the realms of myth and conjecture. Greg does this repeatedly, although his confidence began to wane in the 1850's and, like most Victorians, grew less enthusiastic in the second half of his century. The most enduring expression of Victorian optimism dates from 1837, when Macaulay declared that "an acre in Middlesex is better than a principality in Utopia." The quotation is from his *Edinburgh Review*[33] article on

genius, I should consider his name as deserving never to be mentioned, . . . but with the works of the poet no such danger occurs, and the critic need not be afraid of employing his pen; for the original will continue unimpaired, although his own labours should immediately be consigned to oblivion." (*The Family Shakspere in Eight Volumes*, 5th Edition, [London, 1827], Preface to the First Edition, pp. xv–xvi.) For full vindication of a much maligned man, see the Appendix to Marvin Rosenberg's *The Masks of Othello*, called "A Kind Word for Bowdler" (pp. 244–56).

[32] Houghton, *The Victorian Frame of Mind*, p. 323.

[33] July, 1837, quoted in *Prose of the Victorian Period*, ed. William E. Buckler (Boston, 1958), p. 52.

Francis Bacon, a figure who fascinated early and late Victorians alike.

There is always the danger that a writer who wants to reverse the judgment of his predecessors, or replace their perspective, will distort his evidence. The simplest way to do this, it seems to me, is by selecting representatives of the undercurrent or countercurrent of tradition. Whatever one body of men has ever expressed is invariably contraverted by another. Through discriminating selection of these unrepresentative historical figures, one may readily present to posterity a view wholly inconsistent with what representative men then thought. This "representative (or misrepresentative) reconstruction" is itself a bias and one, for example, with which a representative Marxist like A. T. Kettle must argue. But it seems to me the most useful bias from which to examine Victorian Shakespeare criticism. G. M. Young provides a justification for this method. I cite with pleasure:

> Philosophies of History are many, and all of them are wrecked on the truth that in the career of mankind the illuminated passages are so brief, so infrequent, and still for the most part so imperfectly known, that we have not the materials for a valid induction. Of historic method, indeed, nothing wiser has ever been said than a word which will be found in Gibbon's youthful *Essay on the Study of Literature*. Facts, the young sage instructs us, are of three kinds: those which prove nothing beyond themselves, those which serve to illustrate a character or explain a motive, and those which dominate the system and move its springs. But if we ask what this system is, which provides our canon of valuation, I do not believe we can yet go further than to say, it is the picture as the individual observer sees it.[34]

In an effort to avoid distortion, I propose to look closely at the three figures—Dowden, Swinburne, and Bradley—whom David Nichol Smith cited as the principal Victorian critics.[35] Although

---

[34] G. M. Young, *Victorian England*, pp. 273–74.

his three figures are, properly speaking, late Victorians, and although Swinburne and Dowden held very different views, his selection was entirely fitting. These men, around whom others may be grouped, truly represent the mainstream of later Victorian criticism.

I propose to scant Bradley, not because he is in any way unsuitable to my purpose but simply because he is too well known. Besides, the publication of his lectures dates from 1904, somewhat beyond the limits of our period, although Bradley acknowledged his debt to Victorian criticism:

> I believe the criticism of *King Lear* which has influenced me most is that in Prof. Dowden's *Shakspere, his Mind and Art* (though, when I wrote my lectures, I had not read that criticism for many years); and I am glad that this acknowledgment gives me the opportunity of repeating in print an opinion which I have often expressed to students, that anyone entering on the study of Shakespeare, and unable or unwilling to read much criticism, would do best to take Prof. Dowden for his guide.[36]

Arguments about Bradley have been drawn out for a good quarter century. Now, coincident with the passing of *Scrutiny*, Bradley's great genius is being recognized once more and with it the validity of moral and ethical interpretation. The newest volume of *Shakespeare Criticism 1935–1960*, in the Oxford World's Classics, points this changing fashion. J. I. M. Stewart introduces Bradley in the first paragraph of his contribution entitled "Shakespeare's Men and Their Morals," and then quite casually he parenthetically reaffirms the precedence of *Shakespearean Tragedy*. His sixth paragraph begins:

> Bradley came to crown this situation [dealing with Shakespeare's

---

[35] *Shakespeare Criticism, 1623–1840*, p. xxi. Smith also says that the Victorians show "no conspicuous change in attitude and purpose" from "Carlyle's paean" (1840) and that the reader will judge for himself.

[36] A. C. Bradley, *Shakespearean Tragedy*, p. 430.

creations as moral beings]. He brought to it first his genius (for the writer of the best book on Shakespeare must, I think be allowed that) and secondly a great interest in the philosophy of tragedy. For Bradley, as for Johnson, Shakespeare's heroes are men. But now they are men realized for us, in the two-hours traffic of the stage, in the richest and most delicate psychological detail.[37]

Stewart's next paragraph brings us full circle from the "mischievous" Bradley, whose pernicious influence Leavis still scented in academic criticism: "Perhaps he [Bradley] is a little too good to be true, this serene and timeless Shakespeare, with Aristotle and Hegel in one pocket, the Oxford of 1904 in the other, and the sacred coal ever at his lips. But only perhaps—for who can tell? Is there anything, then, *demonstrably* wrong with Bradley?"[38] Helen Gardner, in the *Times Literary Supplement* number devoted to Shakespeare, relates this concern with *people* to growing interest in the Victorian novel:

> The reaction that is apparent against a criticism that ignored the characters to concentrate on themes and images, and sought for inner meanings beneath the level of plot has gone with the movement of younger critics towards the study of the novel and the welcome return to critical favour of Dickens. But mere reversion to the old way of character study is not possible. The new approach will have to stand upon the shoulders of its predecessor and use many of the weapons it forged. I think Miss Mary Lascelles in her book on *Measure for Measure* (1952) voiced what is increasingly being felt to be a true view when she wrote:
>
>> For all its disadvantages, however; for all the perils of misunderstanding with which it is beset; the study of the characters in their relations with one another—here, conditioned by the given story, there, developing free of it—remains the right

---

[37] J. I. M. Stewart, "Shakespeare's Men and Their Morals," in *Shakespeare Criticism 1935–1960*, ed. Anne Ridler, p. 292.

[38] *Shakespeare Criticism 1935–1960*, p. 293.

approach; and its alternative, a pursuit of phantoms; of inner and innermost meanings derived from word or phrase that has been isolated from its context, of an intention not demonstrably the dramatist's.[39]

Bradley lived on to 1935, long enough for him to catch the first three years of *Scrutiny*. One wonders whether he was among that magazine's charter subscribers, but then, like Swinburne and Stewart, he was an Oxford man.

David Nichol Smith called *Shakespearean Tragedy* "the last great representative of nineteenth-century criticism," and Professor Stewart affirms it "the best book on Shakespeare." I think Dr. Johnson's Preface might share the palm, but at all events Bradley is fitting culmination to the ethical tradition within Victorian Shakespeare studies.

Before this history moves on to Dowden, some mention should be made of Richard Green Moulton's *Shakespeare as a Dramatic Artist: A Popular Illustration of the Principles of Scientific Criticism*, first published in 1885. Moulton would be better known today had not Bradley surpassed him. The achievement of *Shakespearean Tragedy* rests on many insights articulated by Moulton some two decades earlier. These were given relatively wide publicity through their first appearance as papers read before the New Shakspere Society.

Moulton, as his subtitle indicates, attempted to create a science of aesthetics. His Introduction, subtitled "Plea for an Inductive Science of Literary Criticism," is in the spirit of that new criticism which attempted to reconcile scientific method with moral responsibility. Moulton felt that he had reconciled the traditional sense of justice with those laws of nature his contemporaries were then uncovering at so fast a rate. Moulton's frame of reference explains the limitation of this method. He argued that dramatic laws must be

[39] *Times Literary Supplement*, April 23, 1964, p. 335.

derived inductively if they are to have permanent validity and not degenerate into mere opinion:

> It is necessary then to insist upon the strict scientific sense of the term "law" as used of literature and art; and the purging of criticism from the confusion attaching to this word is an essential step in its elevation to the inductive standard. It is a step, moreover, in which it has been preceded by other branches of thought. At one time the practice of commerce and the science of economy suffered under the same confusion: the battle of "free trade" has been fought, the battle of "free art" is still going on. In time it will be recognized that the practice of artists, like the operations of business, must be left to its natural working, and the attempt to impose external canons of taste on artists will appear as futile as the attempt to effect by legislation the regulation of prices.[40]

Moulton was a critic of elegance and sensitivity, but this quotation indicates why his synthesis of science and art would become untenable in the twentieth century. Moulton's book first appeared in 1885, the year Gladstone and free trade were challenged by the imperialist policy of protection (*OED* dates fair trade from 1881). The problem is with us still, but our formulations must be related to differing definitions of art and law. Both Bradley's inductive method and his occasional uncertainty concerning the "laws" of tragedy derive from Moulton, whom he acknowledges only once, in his first note on "Construction in Shakespeare's Tragedies."[41] Moulton's next Shakespeare volume handles more congenial subject matter with less emphasis on science, *The Moral System of Shakespeare: A Popular Illustration of Fiction as the Experimental Side of Philosophy*.[42] Moulton was a Cambridge man who taught literature and religion at the University of Chicago for many years.

[40] Richard G. Moulton, *Shakespeare as A Dramatic Artist: A Popular Illustration of the Principles of Scientific Criticism* (1906), pp. 34–35.

[41] Bradley, p. 405.

[42] London, 1903.

Dowden is less insistently committed to science than Moulton, although an awareness of evolution and philosophy often color his prose. Joyce, for example, would have had more difficulty raising a laugh had he selected the opening of *Shakspere: A Critical Study of His Mind and Art* with its "two modes of apprehending propositions."[43] As we might expect, Dowden opts for real and not abstract knowledge. "To come into close and living relation with the individuality of a poet must be the chief end of our study—to receive from his nature the peculiar impulse and impression which he, best of all, can give."[44] Dowden's critical bent was either influenced by or was itself part of the attempted late Victorian identification with some great individual of which Walter Houghton spoke. In a somewhat irrelevant aside to his chapter on the Roman plays, Dowden himself makes the association and contrasts modern ennui to Elizabethan vigor:

> A time will perhaps come, more favorable to true art than the present, when ideas are less outstanding factors in history than they have been in this century; when thought will be obscurely present in instinctive action and in human emotion, and will vitalize and inspire these joyously rather than tyrannically dominate them. And then men's sympathy with the Elizabethan drama will be more prompt and sure than in our day it can be.[45]

This pre-Lawrencian lament for the instinctual life might have been construed as an example of Dowden's modernism. Instead, like most Victorians, his enthusiasm for personality is taken to confirm that dramatic value and artistic objectivity have been shunted aside for character mongering. Yet Dowden consistently remarked that such was not his purpose. In the second paragraph of his *Shakspere* he warns:

[43] Edward Dowden, *Shakspere: A Critical Study of His Mind and Art*, 3d ed., p. 1. (Hereafter referred to as Dowden, *Shakspere*.)

[44] Dowden, *Shakspere*, p. 2.

[45] Dowden, *Shakspere*, p. 287.

... no experiment will here be made to bring Shakspere before the reader as he spoke and walked, as he jested in his tavern or meditated in his solitude. It is a real apprehension of Shakspere's character and genius which is desired, but not such an apprehension as mere observation of the externals of the man, of his life or of his poetry, would be likely to produce. I wish rather to attain to some central principles of life in him which animate and control the rest, for such there are existent in every man whose life is life in any true sense of the word, and not a mere affair of chance, of impulse, of moods, and of accidents.[46]

In the Preface to the first edition of his *Shakspere*, Dowden tells us that "About half of this volume was read in the form of lectures ('Saturday Lectures in connection with Alexandra College, Dublin') in the Museum Buildings, Trinity College, Dublin, during the spring of the year 1874."[47] Fifteen years later (1889), Dowden published his *Introduction to Shakespeare*. He here restated his theory of a career spanning four distinct phases and once more disclaimed the personal interpretation post-Victorians persist in attributing to him. Since the idea that Shakespeare's work is comprised of successive distinct phases is still very much a part of the critical thinking that despises Victorian standards of judgment, perhaps Dowden should be allowed to state his own case:

Various attempts have been made by Shakespeare scholars to distinguish the successive stages in the development of his genius, and to classify his plays in a series of chronological groups.[48] The latest

[46] Dowden, *Shakspere*, p. 2. This resembles Keats's remark, "A Man's life of any worth is a continuous allegory." The periods under which Dowden organizes his plays are consistent with the way Keats's imagination organized Shakespeare's art. Rarely does Dowden confuse Shakespeare's personal speculations with the designations he attributes to dramatic groupings.

[47] Dowden, *Shakspere*, p. xxi. A remarkable proportion of Victorian Shakespeare criticism originated in adult education lectures. Moulton had been active in university extension work, and Furnivall hoped that his New Shakspere Society would popularize the "Poet" with working people.

attempt is that of a learned French Orientalist, who is also a well-informed student of English literature, M. James Darmesteter.[49] It is substantially identical with what I had myself proposed, a division of the total twenty or twenty-five years of Shakespeare's authorship into four periods of unequal length, to which I had given names intended to lay hold of the student's memory, names which, without being fanciful, should be striking and easy to bear in mind. The earliest period I called "In the Workshop," meaning by this the term of apprenticeship and tentative effort. The years which immediately followed, during which Shakespeare, though a master of his art, dwelt on the broad surface of human life, years represented by the best English histories and some of the brightest comedies, I named "In the World." To indicate the third period, that of the serious, dark, or bitter comedies, and those great tragedies in which the poet makes his searching inquisition into evil, the title "Out of the Depths" served sufficiently well. Finally, for the closing period, when the romantic comedies, at once grave and glad—Cymbeline, The Winter's Tale, The Tempest—were written, I chose the name "On the Heights," signifying thereby that in these exquisite plays Shakespeare had attained an altitude from which he saw human life in a clear and solemn vision, looking down through a pellucid atmosphere upon human joys and sorrows with a certain aloofness or disengagement, yet at the same time with a tender and pathetic interest.

[48] Malone was the first to attempt this series, but its full development is logically a product of the Victorian attempt to rationalize and number the natural universe.

[49] It would have been more appropriate had Dowden cited one of the many Germans working simultaneously along the same lines, but Dowden's own bias was toward the French. The *Jahrbuch der deutschen Shakespeare-Gesellschaft* (Berlin, 1865–71, Weimar, 1872–   ) is rich in statistical studies as well as in the application of biblical higher criticism to the body of Shakespeare's work. Members of the New Shakspere Society were naturally sympathetic to German scholarship and at Furnivall's death in 1910, researchers in both countries hoped that his activity had helped to create mutual understanding in the two countries most deeply inspired by Shakespeare's genius. German devotion to Shakespeare was confirmed during World War II when the *Jahrbuch* continued to appear.

After this clear and, at least to one reader, unobjectionable summary of his own position, Dowden reiterates his warning against a personal transference of these qualities to the historical Shakespeare:

> . . . the reader should be on his guard against the notion that at any time either what we now term "pessimism" or what we term "optimism" formed the creed, or any portion of the creed, of Shakespeare.[50]

The first three of these periods were named in *Shakspere: A Critical Study of His Mind and Art.* "On the Heights" made its first appearance two years later in the *Shakspere* literature primer.[51] Of course no organization into periods would have been possible without the classification and dating which was then going on. Without the comparative method Fleay championed, Victorian critics would have remained almost as uncertain as Coleridge whether *The Tempest* was an early or late play, and it would have been impossible for Dowden to attempt the distribution so gracefully recorded in these paragraphs.

Dowden's serene Shakespeare endured about a quarter of a century. G. Lytton Strachey's "Shakespeare's Final Period" appeared in August, 1904[52] and postulated what might be called the psychotic Shakespeare. It is moot whether Strachey was expressing his usual perversity toward things Victorian or genuinely detected a radical weakening in Shakespeare's final plays. In 1894, Barrett Wendell of Harvard had concluded his discussion of *The Tempest* with the following three sentences: "His faculty of creating character, as distinguished from constructing it, is gone. All his power fails to make his great poem spontaneous, easy, inevitable. Like *Cymbeline* it remains a Titanic effort; and, in an artist like Shak-

---

[50] Edward Dowden, *Introduction to Shakespeare*, pp. 52–53.

[51] Dowden, *Shakspere*, p. 60.

[52] *Independent Review*, III, 405–18.

spere, effort implies creative decadence,—the fatal approach of growing age."[53]

It was this Strachey essay to which T. S. Eliot alluded in his Shakespeare Association Lecture for 1927, beginning: "The last few years have witnessed a number of recrudescences of Shakespeare. There is the fatigued Shakespeare, a retired Anglo-Indian, presented by Mr. Lytton Strachey . . ."—a characterization which may help explain the final days of the British raj in princely India.[54]

The other general objection recorded against Victorian critics was their neglect of text in the search for meaning. Poetry was lost sight of, the newer critics agreed. Now this is an objection Swinburne himself made in the course of his controversy with the New Shakspere Society. His argument will receive a full hearing because it turned on a consideration still relevant nearly a hundred years after the event. But the immediate issue is Dowden's insensitivity to verse in his preoccupation with periods. Dowden himself was an accomplished poet, and what he says about the growth of Shakespeare's verse cannot, I think, be faulted:

As he grew to be a master of his craft the poet came to feel that rhyme rather interrupted than aided the expression of dramatic feeling; having employed rhyme at first freely, and then with reserve, he finally discarded it altogether. At the same time his blank verse underwent various changes, which may all be summed up in the general statement that it became less mechanical and more vital, less formally regular and more swift, subtle and complex—complex not with the intricacy of mechanical arrangement but with the mystery and the movement of life. The flow of the verse became freer; it paused less frequently at the close of the line; it ran into subtly modulated periods; it adapted itself to the expression of every varying mood of feeling; it overleaped the allotted ten syllables, or gathered itself up into a narrower space

[53] Barrett Wendell, *William Shakspere: A Study in Elizabethan Literature*, p. 377.
[54] T. S. Eliot, *Shakespeare and the Stoicism of Seneca*, p. 3.

73

as the movement of passion required; it was no longer the deco-
rated raiment but rather the living body of the idea.[55]

These three sentences are themselves an exercise in style wherein
the author accommodates grammar to the tenor of his argument.
New criticism in the 1920's and 1930's moved on from Dowden to
explain just how verse became swift, subtle, and complex with life.

Dowden of course did not always maintain the distinction between drama and personality he set himself. Of Shakespeare's final
period, he can write something quite personal but, at the same time,
unobjectionable: "In the latest plays of Shakspere the sympathetic
reader can discern unmistakably a certain abandonment of the common joy of the world, a certain remoteness from the usual pleas-
ures and sadnesses of life, and, at the same time, all the more, this
tender bending over those who are, like children, still absorbed
in their individual joys and sorrows."[56] What came to grate
twentieth-century critics was a different kind of character interpretation that smells of Podsnap. Indexed under "Shakspere, on
communism" we find the kind of personal interest Dowden hoped
to avoid: "In Shakspere's late play, *The Tempest*, written when he
was about to retire for good to his Stratford home, he indulges in a
sly laugh at the principles of communism. He who had earned the
New Place, and become a landed gentleman by years of irksome
toil, did not see that he was bound to share his tenements and lands
with his less industrious neighbours."[57] (The sacredness of private
property is a cornerstone of Victorian liberalism, but no one feared
communism like the German Shakespeare critic.) Dowden is characteristically mild in comparison with Gervinus, whose summation
affirms in part that "We must read in Richard II. with what
earnestness he insists upon the sacredness of property, and in
Troilus and Othello with what rigour he maintains the strict ob-

[55] Dowden, *Introduction to Shakespeare*, p. 55.
[56] Dowden, *Shakspere*, p. 369.
[57] Dowden, *Shakspere*, pp. 289–90.

servance of family, in order that we may understand how infinite is the gap which separates Shakespeare from the political free-thinkers of the present day. . . . whither the equalisation and prosperity of communism would lead he has made most plain in Cade's revolution."[58] Dowden quotes Bagehot on the Cade passage: "You will generally find that when a 'citizen' is mentioned, he does or says something absurd," to demur with a note of his own: "Not always. See, for example, King Richard III, *Act* ii., *Sc.* 3, where a 'divine instinct' informing men's minds of coming danger moves in the breasts of the citizens."[59]

The Victorian habit of interpretation should be seen in its twentieth-century context as well. Every list of the ten most important Shakespeare studies in the twentieth century would include *Shakespeare's Imagery and What It Tells Us*, by Caroline F. E. Spurgeon. What it tells us about Shakespeare goes beyond anything in Dowden: "These, then, as I see them, are the five outstanding qualities of Shakespeare's nature—sensitiveness, poise, courage, humour and wholesomeness—balancing, complementing and supporting each other. If he is abnormally sensitive, he is also unusually courageous, mentally and spiritually. . . . He is indeed himself in many ways in character what one can only describe as Christ-like. . . ."[60]

The great Edmund Chambers was more Victorian in his moderation while searching out a heroic Shakespeare to guide England. His *Shakespeare: A Survey* opens with a sonnet dated 1916:

Shakespeare, we need thy solace in this day;
Not for the bugles blown about our skies . . . .
Not these! but malice up and down our streets,
The babbling tongues, the minds that cannot hold

---

[58] Gervinus, *Commentaries*, pp. 924–25.

[59] Dowden, *Shakspere*, pp. 291–92.

[60] Caroline Spurgeon, *Shakespeare's Imagery and What It Tells Us*, pp. 206–207.

An equal course till Time's full circle meets,
The fretful pens shod with an egoist's gold.
Master, deep read in man's fantastic brain,
Smile from thy sculptured stone, and leave us sane.[61]

Later in life, Dowden retreated from interpretation and tended to stress comparative scholarship. Lily Bess Campbell, in her Preface to *Shakespeare's Tragic Heroes*,[62] praises the scientific spirit displayed in "Elizabethan Psychology," an article Dowden wrote for the *Atlantic Monthly* in 1907.[63] She contrasts Bradley's interpretive criticism with the modern scientific method employed by Dowden in his *Atlantic Monthly* piece, in which he catalogues and compares various Elizabethan writings in order to determine what Shakespeare and his contemporaries really meant by their use of obsolete or unfamiliar terms. But far from being modern, Dowden in his old age was returning to the technique Fleay had employed at the inception of the New Shakspere Society some thirty-five years earlier. All through the 1880's and 1890's, before his interest turned to Egyptology, Fleay insisted that the way to understand what Shakespeare meant was through the exhaustive tabulation of what his contemporaries meant by the same or analogous terms. Fleay's strident emotional insistence on scientific certainty led him to numerical tabulation with its illusion of exactitude.[64] Other members of the New Shakspere Society demurred, and some twenty years' experimentation taught the Victorians that analogies are approximation whereas other explanations than the desired one may account for any given phenomena. Yet every year books and

[61] E. K. Chambers, *Shakespeare: A Survey.*
[62] Lily Bess Campbell, p. v.
[63] Pages 388–99.
[64] Number continues to encroach on language but certainty persistently eludes the scientific critic. Writing only a decade apart, Caroline Spurgeon (*Shakespeare's Imagery* 1935) and Edward Armstrong (*Shakespeare's Imagination* London, 1946) tell us very different things about Shakespeare, though both employ a technique introduced and popularized by the New Shakspere Society.

articles are published proving that Shakespeare derived some idea or metaphor or turn of plot from a host of hitherto obscure Elizabethan documents.

Fleay was not long a member of the New Shakspere Society. Furnivall announced his retirement in July, 1874, after a series of controversial letters in the public columns of the *Athenaeum* (May, 1874) embarrassing to the New Shakspere Society. But he was indirectly responsible for the fact that the 1870's were enlivened by yet another example of the scholarly virulence which periodically overtakes Shakespeare studies. Swinburne was naturally at the center of it, and in a review of his *Study of Shakespeare* (London, 1880), the high-minded *Westminster Review* observed: "Is that all you have learnt out of Shakspeare—to . . . revile one another like a parcel of fish-fags? Milton was of opinion that the object of reading and of studying was to improve our moral conduct; but the object of studying Shakspeare would seem to be to deteriorate it. Shakspearians are very much like religious people. In their zeal for their god they forget all his commandments."[65] Since the controversy turned on a question not yet resolved and still relevant, it should repay examination in detail.

Cecil Lang, in the first volume of *The Swinburne Letters*,[66] describes Furnivall in the following capsule biography:

Frederick James Furnivall (1825–1910), the indefatigable scholar who founded the Early English Text [1864], Chaucer [1868], Ballad [1868], New Shakspere [1874],[67] Shelley [1886], Browning [1881], and Wyclif [1881] societies. Moreover, he was a pioneer in the Working Men's College, a grand-

[65] *Westminster Review*, April, 1880, p. 616.

[66] Cecil Y. Lang, ed., *The Swinburne Letters*.

[67] The year 1874 marks the founding also of Furnivall's Sunday Shakspere Society. This was designed for working people who would not be able, in the nature of things, to participate in the Friday-night proceedings of the middle-class New Shakspere Society.

parent of the *Oxford English Dictionary*, and, in addition, one of the most quarrelsome men in the history of letters, though in his feud with Swinburne in the seventies he found his equal.[68]

He was, moreover, a man very much like Swinburne; about the same age (Swinburne's dates are 1837–1909), both reacted against the rigidity of their fathers, both jettisoned received religion, and both attempted to retrieve some humanist substitute for what was no longer acceptable in the faith of their fathers. They were peppery and unconventional, and it is sad to watch men fight so hard who had so much in common. There is a great deal on which both agreed, but their dispute, in its growing ferocity, came to stress the points of disagreement and degenerated into meaningless name calling. Most commentators are at a loss to account for the mudslinging. But one of Swinburne's earliest letters to Furnivall,[69] dated February 7, 1868, long before the Shakespeare controversy, discusses Elizabethan birching and flagellation and thanks Furnivall for sending him a volume which alluded to the subject, inscribed "Algernon Swinburne, Esq. with the Editor's compts. and Thanks, 28 Jany. 1868." It is just possible that latent homosexual associations stored up at this time erupted in verbal hostilities a decade later.

Furnivall, like Swinburne, was a man of great courage despite his quick temper, and the way he faced news that he was slowly dying of cancer can be described only as heroic. The day-to-day flavor of the man's impetuosity comes through in Caroline Spurgeon's recollection of how he founded one of his learned societies:

> The way in which this all-conquering power carried him through his own work is well illustrated in the account he used to give of the founding of the Browning Society. Some lady said to him one afternoon, casually, "I wonder you don't found a Browning

[68] Lang, I, 153 n.
[69] Lang, I, 289–310.

Society, for Browning's works are every bit as obscure and un-
decipherable as any of your Early English texts." "You are quite
right," was the Doctor's reply, and on the way home he bought a
pound's worth of stamps, sat up all night writing letters to suit-
able people on the subject, and by the evening of the following day
the first members had joined.[70]

At the time of the controversy, Furnivall himself was not a Shakespeare scholar but rather, as his other accomplishments indicate, an
organizer of scholars. Indeed, the ideas he came to hold (broadly
speaking, those of Dowden as quoted in the preceding pages) were
at one time compatible with Swinburne's. When they came to dis-
agree, it was over method. In a letter written while they were still
on good terms, Swinburne said (February 24, 1875) in regard to
the essays out of which he was to work up his 1880 study on Shakespeare: ". . . but I shall not attempt in my study to determine (for
instance) the precedence of Love's Labour's Lost or the Comedy
of Errors—merely to arrange them in classes or periods according
to style, metre, etc. and *then* examine the special influences of that
period. I believe this has been done before by Gervinus. . . ."[71]
(Furnivall's own essay on Gervinus was originally dated September 16, 1874.) During this period both men were working along
not dissimilar lines—Swinburne tentatively looking for structural
and aesthetic continuity (as Wilson Knight was to do), and Furnivall's continuity rooted in chronology.

In its most productive form, the controversy between Furnivall
and Swinburne turned on whether criticism was science or art.
Could any judgment be formulated with scientific exactitude so as
to satisfy all reasonable men, or was the science of aesthetics in-

[70] Caroline F. E. Spurgeon in *Frederick James Furnivall: A Volume of
Personal Record*, p. 184. Doubtless T. J. Wise had his own reasons for expediting
formation of a Browning Society that would attempt facsimile reproductions of
the poet's early works.
[71] Lang, III, 19.

extricably linked with personal preference?[72] Fleay had attempted a science of evaluation or at least a scientific method which told *him* who wrote what. By parceling out Shakespeare's better-known plays among various Elizabethans—for example, he clearly saw Ben Jonson's hand in *Julius Caesar*—Fleay employed the apparatus of scientific method to annihilate Shakespeare's character along with his originality. His use of science was like that of other Victorian materialists, who sought to reduce the role of personality by subsuming more of the natural universe under law. Fleay's activities are therefore one current in the antiheroic mainstream of Victorian thought. This process of disintegration continued well into our own century.[73] One reaction against it is the growing mid-twentieth-century insistence on the integrity of the Shakespeare canon and the growing belief that one man—William Shakespeare—wrote the plays attributed to him by Heminge and Condell in the "Epistle to the Great Variety of Readers."[74]

The authorship of *The First Part of King Henry VI* is a good case in point. Because the writing is relatively poor, critics have tended to attribute the authorship elsewhere. Andrew Cairncross, the editor of the New Arden edition,[75] devotes much of his Introduction to the "destruction of those that went before him." He concludes, "In short, the play bears the stamp of a single mind in the organization of material, in its adaptation to the exposition of a grand central design extending beyond the play itself, and in the reinforcement of the whole by a body of subsidiary devices and

[72] Moulton's *Shakespeare as a Dramatic Artist*, comprising many essays which first appeared as papers read to Furnivall's New Shakspere Society, is the most thoroughgoing attempt to negotiate an art-science synthesis.

[73] John Mackinnon Robertson (1856–1933) was the most prominent "disintegrator." The problem of authenticity is discussed by Edmund Chambers in his 1924 British Academy lecture called *The Disintegration of Shakespeare* (*Proceedings* of the British Academy 1924–25, pp. 89–108).

[74] Preliminary matter, Folio, 1623.

[75] London, 1962.

ideas, to create a highly popular play in an original form."[76] Cairncross does not see Fleay's work as part of a scientific spirit imposing determined forms on the individual genius of Shakespeare. He says elsewhere:

> The main trend of eighteenth- and nineteenth-century criticism was to doubt Shakespeare's sole authorship of *I Henry VI*. It became part of the Shakespeare "mythos" that anything unworthy of his genius or repulsive to the sensibilities of the critic's time should be removed from the canon, and fathered on some alternative writer, or even a "symposium" of writers, with Shakespeare possibly adding a few scenes or revising a whole. In *I Henry VI*, "the revolting treatment of Joan," and the "mean and prosaical" style were sufficient grounds, along with two or three shreds of contemporary evidence and some "echoes" and inconsistencies in the play, for an elaborate theory involving the part authorship of Greene, Marlowe, and Nashe, or some of them.[77]

Narrowing things down a bit, Hilda M. Hulme argues in *Explorations in Shakespeare's Language* that two of the most brilliant textual emendations constitute unwarranted tampering. She says of Hanmer's "spaniel'd" for the Folio's "pannelled" in the lines:

> The hearts
> That pannelled me at heeles, to whom I gaue
> Their wishes, do dis-Candie, melt their sweets
> On blossoming Caesar: (*A and C*, IV, xii, ll., 23–26.)

I shall suggest here that in its compression and economy "pannelled" may be considered genuinely Shakespearean and I shall argue my way from clue to clue, showing the stages of the linguist's procedure.[78]

[76] Andrew S. Cairncross, ed., *The First Part of King Henry VI*, Introduction, p. liii.

[77] Cairncross, ed., p. xxviii.

[78] Hilda M. Hulme, *Explorations in Shakespeare's Language*, p. 103.

81

Nor is the most famous emendation secure. Theobald's "his nose was as sharp as a pen, and a babled of green fields" is also to be restored in the quest for authenticity: "I shall try to argue that the description as given in the folio—'our only relevant authority' in the words of Sir Walter Greg—is meaningful, and that to allow Theobald to alter the original text is merely to prefer the unambiguous sentiment of a most skilful eighteenth-century editor to the complex artistry of the greatest Elizabethan dramatist."[79]

Furnivall's position was more humane and complex than Fleay's or Miss Hulme's. Like Swinburne, he wanted to marry poetic insight to the new scientific disciplines, and his controversy with Swinburne foreshadowed the growing alienation of science from art. Tennyson is commonly said to have been the last national poet who embraced both worlds—or the two cultures, as we more commonly phrase it today. Wordsworth had of course foreseen the problem as early as 1800 and attempted to encourage a poetic treatment of scientific discoveries:

And thus the Poet, prompted by this feeling of pleasure [Wordsworth's first cause], which accompanies him through the whole course of his studies, converses with general nature, with affections akin to those which, through labour and length of time, the Man of science has raised up in himself, by conversing with those particular parts of nature which are the object of his studies. . . . If the labours of Men of science should ever create any material revolution, direct or indirect, in our condition, and in the impressions which we habitually receive, the Poet will sleep then no more than at present; he will be ready to follow the steps of the Man of science, not only in those general indirect effects, but he will be

---

[79] Hulme, p. 134. Miss Hulme is interesting because she argues for the integrity of the "unimproved" text, as Swinburne or Leavis might, but on the basis of scientific (linguistic) not aesthetic evidence. The unusual definitions she applies to Elizabethan words are important because it means that if ever bibliographic and aesthetic critics agree on a text, Shakespeare will still elude us so long as differing meanings are assigned to words in his plays.

at his side, carrying sensation into the midst of the objects of the science itself. The remotest discoveries of the Chemist, the Botanist, or the Mineralogist, will be as proper objects of the Poet's art as any upon which it can be employed, if the time should ever come when these things shall be familiar to us, and the relations under which they are contemplated by the followers of these respective sciences shall be manifestly and palpably material to us as enjoying and suffering beings.[80]

The tone of this reminds us that Wordsworth was born in 1770. Pope would have found it unobjectionable. Wordsworth is surprisingly more accommodating to the scientific method than the liberal Keats was to be a decade later. *Lamia* is antiscientific with a vengeance:

> Do not all charms fly
> At the mere touch of cold philosophy?
> There was an awful rainbow once in heaven:
> We know her woof, her texture; she is given
> In the dull catalogue of common things.
> Philosophy will clip an Angel's wings,
> Conquer all mysteries by rule and line,
> Empty the haunted air, and gnomed mine—
> Unweave a rainbow, as it erewhile made
> The tender-person'd Lamia melt into a shade.[81]

At all events, after Tennyson the Victorian synthesis crumbled; interpretation seemed impossible, and the two traditions went their separate ways. Furnivall tried to rely on Tennyson to provide the aesthetic component in his new criticism, and his happiest moment occurred when Tennyson's judgment complemented Fleay's scientific results. This all too rare circumstance occurred when Fleay and Tennyson agreed as to which parts of *Pericles* were Shake-

[80] *The Complete Poetical Works of Wordsworth.* Preface to "Lyrical Ballads," p. 795.
[81] *Lamia*, Part II, ll. 229–38. *The Poetical Works of John Keats*, ed. H. W. Garrod, p. 212.

speare's. Then, Furnivall remarked, "The independent confirmation of the poet-critic's result by the metrical-test-worker's process is most satisfactory and interesting . . . and should give us confidence in the metrical tests so used."[82]

Swinburne alone seems to have recognized that Fleay's method would annihilate the individual genius of Shakespeare or of any man. Indeed, Fleay's work leads straight to E. E. Stoll, who saw Shakespeare as the natural product of his times, devoid of personal integrity or logical coherence, whose characters respond to one another not out of innermost needs but because the laws of Elizabethan dramaturgy demand precisely the arbitrary responses Hamlet, Othello, or Lear invariably make. Of course Fleay's contemporaries, with the exception of a rare genius like Swinburne, did not see scientific investigation tending in this antiheroic direction. To other members of the New Shakspere Society, Fleay was merely purifying Shakespeare, making the hero more truly heroic through the elimination of whatever dross had accumulated round his feet. To them, far from circumscribing the hero, Fleay's work enlarged his dimensions. A. J. Ellis, of the Philological Society, said: "Although outsiders might imagine that Mr Fleay's numerical treatment of Shakspere was a poetical desecration, he foresaw that it gave a means, independent of mere subjective feeling, for separating the feet of clay from the heart of gold, so that we should not be idolizing as Shakspere's what he never wrote."[83]

This may be the appropriate moment to say something about a

[82] New Shakspere Society, *Transactions 1874*, p. 253.

[83] New Shakspere Society, *Transactions 1874*, p. 19. Ellis was a prominent mathematician, one of the men who Furnivall hoped would mediate the arts-science split. Charles Babbage (1792–1871), father of the computer and public-spirited eccentric, might have organized New Shakspere Society research more systematically than anyone. An essay, "On Tables of the Constants of Nature and Art," appeared in the *Annual Report of the Board of Regents of the Smithsonian Institution for 1856*. Unfortunately, Babbage died a few years before Furnivall's society got under way. His autobiography, *Passages from the Life of a Philosopher*, makes mention of neither Furnivall nor Shakespeare.

freak of scholarship that flourished most prominently in the Victorian period, the Shakespeare-Bacon controversy. The proponents of Baron Verulam generally base their argument on science as would no doubt have pleased the author of *De Augmentis Scientiarum*. Their experiments are generally inconclusive verse test rather than an examination of Elizabethan culture, but they are scientific in a philosophical sense, for they deny the individuality of Shakespeare and transfer his achievements to a more probable and logical candidate. This of course was not what Ellis meant, but the scientific method cuts both ways.

The "Disintegrators," men like Fleay and Robertson, who see the hands of other Elizabethans in the plays of the First Folio, should not be confused with the Baconians, who substitute another author for the plays attributed to Shakespeare. Robertson made this clear in 1913 by publishing his *Baconian Heresy: A Confutation*. The most distinguished Baconian was that late Victorian Sigmund Freud. His adherence can be explained on the grounds that even the most sympathetic observer of a foreign culture is more severely handicapped than he realizes by the language barrier. I quote most of a long footnote added to his *Autobiographical Study* in 1935 for the sake of interdisciplinary insight. Strictly speaking, Freud was not a Baconian—his candidate turned out to be the seventeenth Earl of Oxford, Edward de Vere (1550–1604). Possibly Freud recognized the neurotic obsessional characteristics of the orthodox Baconians and prudently declined to associate himself with them:

I no longer believe that William Shakespeare the actor from Stratford was the author of the works which have so long been attributed to him. Since the publication of J. T. Looney's volume *"Shakespeare" Identified* [1929], I am almost convinced that in fact Edward de Vere, Earl of Oxford, is concealed behind this pseudonym.—[When, in 1935, the English translator received the draft of this additional footnote, he was so much taken aback that he wrote to Freud asking him to reconsider it—not on the ground of the truth or otherwise of the theory, but of the effect the note was likely to have on the average English reader, particularly in view of the unfortunate name of the author of the book referred to. Freud's reply was most forbearing, as an excerpt from a translation of his letter will show. The letter is dated August 29, 1935. ". . . As regards the Shakespeare-Oxford note, your proposal puts me in the unusual situation of showing myself as an opportunist. I cannot understand the English attitude to this question: Edward de Vere was certainly as good an Englishman as Will Shakspere. But since the matter is so remote from analytic interest, and since you set so much store on my being reticent, I am ready to cut out the note, or merely to insert a sentence such as 'For particular reasons I no longer wish to lay emphasis on this point.' Decide on this yourself. On the other hand, I should be glad to have the whole note retained in the American edition. The same sort of narcissistic defence need not be feared over there. . . ."][84]

One of the best "separators" of Shakespeare from Bacon is the free-association test suggested by Furnivall and picked up by Miss Spurgeon in *Shakespeare's Imagery and What It Tells Us*.[85] Interestingly, this test was recently confirmed quite outside the usual academic world through an image Miss Spurgeon neglected to catalogue.

The late George Arents could be persuaded to buy almost any rare English book with a reference to tobacco. He owned a great many works by Francis Bacon, for Bacon often refers to smoking. The New York book trade knew that Arents would pay handsomely for Shakespeare, but despite their incentive and the most refined ingenuity of determined merchants, Arents could never be con-

---

[84] Brackets are the editor's, not mine. *The Standard Edition of the Complete Psychological Works of Sigmund Freud* (London, 1959), XX, 63–64 n.

[85] Spurgeon, pp. 16–29 and charts I–IV.

vinced that a volume of Shakespeare belonged in his collection of works on tobacco.[86]

The Baconians were beneath Swinburne's contempt—and he never mentions them—but, far more clearly than Ellis, he understood the dehumanizing implications of Fleay's method. Like Tennyson, whose work he generally admired, Swinburne was deeply permeated by the scientific habit of mind. Where Tennyson attempted to reconcile science and the Anglican tradition, Swinburne tried to revitalize the myths of Greek antiquity as a replacement for Christianity compatible with modern science. The depth of Swinburne's hostility to Christianity can be best understood by examining the poignant letter from Watts-Dunton to Swinburne's sole surviving sister explaining why the burial service could not be read over Swinburne's grave.[87]

In the 1870's, Swinburne had a more immediate pique against the Reverend Frederick Fleay. Citing objections to his method, Fleay inadvertently (for he seems to have been a man without personal malice) belittled Swinburne: "But is not metre too delicate a thing to be put in the balance or crucible in this way? . . . Can we always distinguish Tennyson from his imitators? and is not the trick of Swinburne's melody easily acquired and reproduced?"[88] Swinburne retaliated in the first installment of "The Three Stages of Shakespeare," two essays which first appeared in the *Fortnightly Review*[89] and formed the body of his 1880 publication *A Study of*

[86] For an exhaustive survey of tobacco in English literature, see *Tobacco: Its History Illustrated by the Books, Manuscripts, and Engravings in the Library of George Arents, Jr.* For Shakespeare and tobacco, see the Introduction by Jerome Brooks, pp. 65–69. As if fulfilling Parkinson's law, this magnificent collection was presented to the New York Public Library about the time tobacco and cancer were first linked.

[87] Lang, VI, 222, 223.

[88] New Shakspere Society, *Transactions, 1874*, p. 2.

[89] *Fortnightly Review*, May, 1875, pp. 613–32; January, 1876, pp. 24–45. The *Fortnightly Review* had suspended mid-monthly publication without change of title.

Shakespeare. Swinburne indulges his appetite for alliterative vituperation, but he comes to the heart of the matter in due course:

> . . . the fatuity of pedantic ignorance never devised a grosser absurdity than the attempt to separate aesthetic from scientific criticism by a strict line of demarcation, and to bring all critical work under one or the other head of this exhaustive division. Criticism without accurate science of the thing criticised can indeed have no other value than may belong to the genuine record of a spontaneous impression; but it is not less certain that criticism which busies itself only with the outer husk or technical shell of a great artist's work, taking no account of the spirit or the thought which informs it, cannot have even so much value as this.[90]

It is a mistake to assume from this that Swinburne lacked historical perspective or the learning necessary to historical perspective and judgments based on analogy. What he said about Shakespeare is not based on ignorance of other Elizabethan playwrights. Lang writes:

> It could be said of him, as Boswell said of Johnson, that "no man had a more ardent love of literature, or a higher respect for it," but much of his work was done in a field so exclusive that no one not a specialist in the third- and fourth-rate seventeenth-century dramatists (or in Swinburne himself) could feel involved in it, and his standing today would be immeasurably greater if he had employed his limitless energies in propagating only the best that was known and thought in the world rather than in hierarchically ranking forgotten playwrights.[91]

Writing to A. H. Bullen (1875–1920), Abbott's former pupil in the City of London School, editor of Elizabethan texts, and founder of the Shakespeare Head Press (1904), Swinburne said, "I am sincerely gratified to know that my studies on Ford and Chapman did for you something of what Lamb did for me when a

[90] May, 1875, p. 616.
[91] Lang, Introduction, I, xvii.

boy at Eton. My own impression is that every English play in existence down to 1640 must be worth reprinting on extrinsic if not on intrinsic ground."[92]

Fleay answered Swinburne's *Fortnightly Review* piece with an article entitled "Who Wrote Henry VI?" In it, Fleay assumes on Swinburne's part complete ignorance of the Elizabethan theater and tends to confirm that he himself was involved "only with the outer shell or technical husk of a great artist's work." His conclusion could only infuriate Swinburne, directed as it was against "the shallow arrogance of the would-be critic or poet who thinks that his capacity is large enough to serve as a measure of the myriad-minded Shakespeare, or even of the greater among his contemporaries."[93] Swinburne wrote to the editor of the *Athenaeum* demanding that "The profound modesty which so notoriously and invariably distinguishes the thoughtful and diffident suggestions of Mr. Fleay on matters relating to the poetic art should not induce him to suppress the name or names of the greater man or men to whom he alludes."[94] Furnivall, a few years later, denied that Fleay had ever said this—a reporter had taken it down inaccurately, he alleged in the *Academy*.[95] At all events, Furnivall felt his society had been slandered. Fleay modestly retired from public controversy, whereas Furnivall imprudently awaited an opportunity to retaliate.

Swinburne, in all his Shakespeare studies, attempts to maintain the integrity of what we call the Shakespeare canon. In 1879, he was to deny Shakespeare's hand in *Edward III*,[96] a play Furnivall had included in his *Leopold Shakspere*.[97] Now, in the second in-

---

[92] Lang, IV, 279–80. (Letter dated June 19, 1882.)

[93] *Macmillan's Magazine*, November, 1875, p. 62.

[94] Lang, III, 118. Text: *Athenaeum*, Jan. 15, 1876, p. 87.

[95] Jan. 10, 1880, p. 28.

[96] "Note on the Historical Play of King Edward III," *Gentleman's Magazine*, Vol. 249 (July to Dec., 1879), pp. 170–81 and 330–49.

[97] *The Leopold Shakspere: The Poet's Works, in Chronological Order, from*

stallment of his "Three Stages of Shakespeare," (January, 1876), Swinburne denied Fletcher's hand in *Henry VIII*. Since Furnivall had reprinted Spedding's *Who Wrote Henry VIII?*, which explicitly designated Fletcher as the play's principal author, Furnivall construed the two articles as a direct attack. Unfortunately, Swinburne overstepped his ground. Perhaps he too had succumbed to the impression that a "scientific" argument was unanswerable. At all events, he rejected Fletcher's hand in the play by claiming that *Henry VIII* contained none of the triple endings of Fletcher's verse, "so that even by the test of the metre-mongers who would reduce the whole question at issue to a point which might at once be solved by the simple process of numeration the argument in favour of Fletcher can hardly be proved tenable."[98] Furnivall easily demonstrated more than twenty triple endings in the parts of *Henry VIII* attributed to Fletcher, but his letter to the *Academy* is of interest for the response it solicited one week later from Swinburne himself.[99] Entitled " 'King Henry VIII' and the Ordeal by Metre,"[100] it deserves careful attention:

> The question upon which I have for once entered is not, it will be observed, a question of ear but of fingers. . . . A dunce like myself, who measures verse, whether in his reading or writing lesson, by ear and not by finger, is naturally compelled to sit down (if he can) on the lowest form among boys who get up their Euclid by the simple process of committing it to memory; for it must by this time be known even to the poor votaries of an in-

---

the Text of Professor Delius (London, 1877). The volume was dedicated to Queen Victoria's youngest son, and included a long preface by Furnivall which was made up principally from his introduction to Gervinus' *Commentaries*. For changes in Swinburne's position, see his *Study of Shakespeare*, pp. 81–94, as against his second article, "The Three Stages of Shakespeare," *Fortnightly Review*, Jan., 1876, pp. 24–25.

[98] "The Three Stages of Shakespeare," *Fortnightly Review*, Jan., 1876, p. 41.

[99] "Mr. Swinburne and Mr. Spedding—Shakspere's 'Henry VIII,' " *Academy* Jan. 8, 1876, p. 35.

[100] Lang, III, 106–11. Published in *Academy* Jan. 15, 1876, pp. 53–55.

ferior form of speech, who believe that verse (the lower form) is distinguished from prose (the higher form) by the faculty of song or verbal music, and who are led by the ear (like the animals they most resemble) to persist in their preference for the lower form over the higher on this most inadequate and absurd account— even to these, I say, it must be notorious that a grand jury of Parnassian pedagogues has established as a primary axiom or postulate that verse, or the music of corresponsive words, in common, I presume, with the other kind of music, does not appeal to the ear, but to the fingers; and by the fingers only, and in no case by the ear, can it be judged.[101]

Swinburne now argues against Fletcher's hand in *Henry VIII* on aesthetic grounds, which he feels cannot be invalidated by scientific computation. This is significant because, as we shall see, his grounds are the same that twentieth-century humanists were to use against the new "scientific" bibliographers who in our own time are scientifically determining what Shakespeare really wrote and what we owe to the vagaries, say, of Compositor B, drunk, blind, or indifferent to the task at hand. In addition, Swinburne has something to say about the problem of Shakespeare's chronology. Because what he says has been resaid in the twentieth century without reference to Swinburne, a further quotation is appropriate:

One word more, and I close a letter which has already overgrown the limits designed for it. Mr. Furnivall taxes me with an attempt to overthrow the established order of Shakspere's plays, which, according to him, is as firmly settled as the order of letters in the alphabet. In my humble opinion this is not, and never can be, the case; but however that may be, the hastiest reader of my notes on the subject might not unreasonably have been expected to bear in mind that from the very beginning I have again and again repudiated all purpose or pretension to do or attempt anything of the kind. It should seem then but useless waste of words to reiterate once again the assurance that my object was not to

[101] *Academy*, Jan. 15, 1876, p. 54.

prove or disprove, set up or upset, any theory whatever concerning the dates of Shakspere's plays, but simply to divide and combine them by rule of poetic order, not by date of actual succession.[102]

This kind of analysis has become the special province of G. Wilson Knight in our own generation, and it is odd to see Knight come down so hard on Swinburne. I cite the second paragraph of Knight's "Principles of Shakespeare Interpretation":

> It is remarkable that the existing mass of Shakespeare criticism should have accomplished so little of positive value in proportion to its bulk. Critic after critic, from poets to academic scholars, has returned to the attack: and reader after reader returns, wisely, not to the critic but to Shakespeare himself, in the theatre or the library. And yet I believe that there has been much waiting for the critics and left undone. This I attribute in many instances to a complete neglect of the poetic quality of the plays; in others, to an easy contentment with, if not overstated, certainly useless, paragraphs of rhetorical and amateurish praise. Swinburne's *Study of Shakespeare* is a case in point.[103]

We will return to Knight shortly. But, as a case in point, here is Swinburne explaining his purpose:

> What I desire to do and design to attempt is a work which has nothing in common with the peremptory pretensions of commentators who seek by dint of positive assertion or endless wrangling to establish as matter of creed what can never be more than matter of opinion; it is to arrange in their several classes the plays of Shakespeare according to their order of poetry, not according to their rate of succession; to rank them by rule of kind, not by computation of priority; to take count of them by style and not by date. This may be a futile, an overweening, unprofitable project;

---

[102] *Academy*, Jan. 15, 1876, p. 54. In *A Study of Shakespeare*, Swinburne said: "It is not, so to speak, the literal but the spiritual order which I have studied to observe and to indicate: the periods which I seek to define belong not to chronology but to art" (p. 16).

[103] G. Wilson Knight, *The Sovereign Flower*, p. 287.

but, rational or irrational, it has no more to do with questions of disputed chronology than the secret of metrical harmony or melody has to do with the casting up of figures or the counting out of syllables.[104]

In a postscript to this long letter, which deserves to be read in its entirety, Swinburne explains that spiritually *Henry VIII* is an early play and concedes quite freely that chronologically it may be one of the latest. He finds it difficult to place because an aging artist often backtracks to the characteristics of his youth.[105] Two sentences of this letter, written in 1876, may have given Lytton Strachey his idea of the degenerating Shakespeare:

> To that second period I therefore ascribe it [*Henry VIII*], subject to the possible future correction of facts as yet unverified, and which, if they were established to-morrow in proofs the most irrefragable, would in no degree affect the soundness or unsoundness of a critical process which aims at separating and rearranging the works of Shakespeare into periods to be measured by aesthetic in place of chronological divisions. Were *King Henry VIII* proved to be, indeed, one of the latest works of Shakespeare . . . it would then be . . . evident that Shakespeare had in his last play fallen back from the final height of his tragic style upon the comparatively immature, tentative, adolescent manner of his earlier labours in the field of national or historical tragedy. . . .[106]

If Strachey did know this letter to the *Academy*, he would not be the first critic to attack the Victorian position with weapons forged in a Victorian arsenal.

Furnivall replied promptly in the *Academy* issue of January 29. He presented further metrical evidence for Fletcher's share in *Henry VIII*, and added confidently: "Now on the question of

[104] Lang, III, 110.

[105] "The reversion to the epic chronicle at the very end of Shakespeare's career is odd. I have sometimes thought that an earlier plot may have been adapted." (Chambers, *William Shakespeare*, I, 497.)

[106] Lang, III, 111.

style. We are only too anxious to meet, and I trust to beat, Mr. Swinburne on his own ground."[107] Again, Furnivall's reply is of interest not for the evidence of triple endings (Swinburne alleged that many of these had the poetic value of double endings) but because of the response he elicited. This time Swinburne's vehicle was the *Examiner*. The April 1 and 15, 1876, issues of that publication carried Swinburne's parody, "A Report of the Proceedings on the First Anniversary Session of the Newest Shakespeare Society,"[108] which later formed the second appendix to his *Study of Shakespeare*.[109]

All of Swinburne's "Report" is worth reading today when scientific criticism is again very strong. But two points stand out. First, like every good parodist, Swinburne carries the New Shakspere Society premise to an illogical and absurd conclusion. He thereby illustrates just how the society is proceeding to annihilate Shakespeare. Here is Furnivall speaking in Swinburne's own words:

> ... Mr. F. proceeded to read his paper on the date of *Othello*, and on the various parts of that play respectively assignable to Samuel Rowley, to George Wilkins, and to Robert Daborne. It was evident that the story of Othello and Desdemona was originally quite distinct from that part of the play in which Iago was a leading figure. This he was prepared to show at some length by means of the weak-ending test, the light-ending test, the double-ending test, the triple-ending test, the heavy-monosyllabic-eleventh-

---

[107] "Mr. Swinburne and Mr. Spedding-Shakspere's 'Henry VIII.' " *Academy*, Jan. 29, 1876, p. 99.

[108] Pages 381–83 and 440–41, respectively. On January 8, the *Examiner* had published a long and laudatory review of *Erechtheus* (pp. 41–43).

[109] The year 1876 saw the anonymous publication in pamphlet form of a clever dramatic satire entitled *Furnivallos Furioso! and "The Newest Shakespeare Society": A Dram-attic Squib of the Period. In Three Fizzes, and Let Off for the Occasion, by the Ghost of Guido Fawkes!* This is generally attributed to one John Jeremiah on the basis of the British Museum Catalogue ascription, but the style is pure Swinburne and quite unlike Jeremiah's other publications extant in New York libraries.

94

syllable-of-the double-ending test, the run-on-line test, and the central-pause test. Of the partnership of other poets in the play he was able to adduce a simpler but not less cogent proof. A member of their Committee said to an objector lately: "To me, there are the handwritings of four different men, the thoughts and powers of four different men, in the play. If you can't see them now, you must wait till, by study, you can. I can't give you eyes." To this argument he (Mr. F.) felt that it would be an insult to their understanding if he should attempt to add another word. Still, for those who were willing to try and learn, and educate their ears and eyes, he had prepared six tabulated statements. . . .[110]

Swinburne also explores the limitation of Fleay's method in demonstrating what truly malicious analogies can be constructed by the interested critic. Here is Swinburne exploring the true significance of *Romeo and Juliet*:

> To the far-reaching eye of Shakespeare it must have seemed natural and inevitable that Paris (Essex) should fall by the hand of Romeo (Burghley) immediately before the monument of the Capulets where their common mistress was interred alive— immediately, that is, before the termination of the Tudor dynasty in the person of Elizabeth, who towards the close of her reign may fitly have been regarded as one already buried with her fathers, though yet living in a state of suspended animation under the influence of a deadly narcotic potion administered by the friends of Romeo—by the partisans, that is, of the Cecilian policy. The Nurse was not less evidently designed to represent the Established Church. Allusions to the marriage of the clergy are profusely scattered through her speeches.[111]

But Fleay's influence was mighty, and every year books and articles appear relating Shakespeare's work, by direct and covert allusion, to the political climate of his England.

[110] Swinburne, *A Study of Shakespeare*, pp. 292–93. The nineteenth century posited different authors for Shakespeare's plays; today's changes are based on faulty transmissions of the text. Higher Bible critics, please take note.

[111] Swinburne, *A Study of Shakespeare*, pp. 312–13.

Finally, Swinburne attempts a criticism of *Shakespeare's Imagery and What It Tells Us* some sixty years before the appearance of Miss Spurgeon's book.[112] Swinburne presents a paper that might almost have been read at one of the New Shakspere Society meetings. Equally, it might have appeared in Miss Spurgeon's book, in the chapter "Shakespeare the Man," where she says: "He had, in short, an excellent eye for a shot, with bowl or with arrow, and loved exercising it. He was, indeed, good at all kinds of athletic sport and exercise, walking, running, dancing, jumping, leaping and swimming."[113] Unfortunately, it does not appear. Here then is Swinburne on Oedipus Shakespeare:

> Mr. E. then brought forward a subject of singular interest and importance—"The lameness of Shakespeare—was it moral or physical?" He would not insult their intelligence by dwelling on the absurd and exploded hypothesis that this expression was allegorical, but would at once assume that the infirmity in question was physical. Then arose the question—In which leg? He was prepared, on the evidence of an early play, to prove to demonstration that the injured and interesting limb was the left. "This shoe is my father," says Launce in the *Two Gentlemen of Verona*; "no, this left shoe is my father; no, no, this left shoe is my mother; nay, that cannot be so neither; yes, it is so, it is so; *it hath the worser sole.*" This passage was not necessary either to the progress of the play or to the development of the character; he believed he was justified in asserting that it was not borrowed from the original novel on which the play was founded; the inference was obvious, that without some personal allusion it must have been as unintelligible to the audience as it had hitherto been to the commentators. His conjecture was confirmed, and the whole subject illustrated with a new light, by the well-known

---

[112] Miss Spurgeon knew Furnivall, and her *Five Hundred Years of Chaucer Criticism and Allusion* (*1357–1900*) (London, 1914–25), a work in the spirit of the New Shakspere Society, was published by the Chaucer Society, which had been founded by Furnivall in 1868.

[113] *Shakespeare's Imagery and What It Tells Us*, pp. 204–205.

line in one of the Sonnets in which the poet describes himself as "made lame by Fortune's dearest spite": a line of which the inner meaning and personal application had also by a remarkable chance been reserved for him (Mr. E.) to discover.[114]

After this the controversy rapidly descended to invective and vituperation. Nothing more was added to the history of Shakespeare criticism. In 1880, Furnivall, in his forewords to a facsimile *Hamlet* Second Quarto, referred to the "porcine vagaries" of "Pigsbrook and Co.," a name formed from the Anglo-Saxon *swin*, "pig," and *burn*, "brook." Swinburne retaliated with "Brothelsdyke," from the Latin *fornix* and *vallum*. Halliwell-Phillipps, who had been a member of both Shakespeare societies, accepted the dedication of Swinburne's book, and in 1881 Furnivall circulated yet another pamphlet entitled *The "Co." of Pigsbrook and Co.* attacking Swinburne and Halliwell-Phillipps too with exceptional ferocity.[115]

Robert Browning, honorary president of the New Shakspere Society, was drawn into the maelstrom; the Duke of Devonshire and many prominent members resigned. Furnivall never recovered, and although his society lingered on another decade, it had become discredited as an unbiased instrument in the furtherance of Shakespeare studies. Furnivall did bring out facsimile quartos of the plays throughout the 1880's and until his Society petered out in 1894; in this activity he may have been encouraged by T. J. Wise, a loyal member of Furnivall's Browning (1881) and Shelley (1886) societies. As director of the Early English

[114] Swinburne, *A Study of Shakespeare*, pp. 291–92. Lillian Hornstein followed up Swinburne's objection to the Furnivall-Spurgeon method in a delightful article entitled "Analysis of Imagery: A Critique of Literary Method," *PMLA*, 57, (1942), pp. 638–53.

[115] The Swinburne-Furnivall papers have been collected by Oscar Maurer in a paper entitled "Swinburne vs. Furnivall: A Case Study in 'Aesthetic' vs. 'Scientific' Criticism," *University of Texas Studies in English*, pp. 86–96, to which I am indebted.

Text Society (EETS) from 1872 until his death in 1910, Furnivall supervised the publication of nearly 250 volumes in Old, Middle, and modern English.

But Swinburne's services to Shakespeare still seem unappreciated. He is usually dismissed as an uncritical impressionist, with a too facile gift for alliterative epithets. G. Wilson Knight, whose criticism owes Swinburne the most, is not surprisingly the most prominent of Swinburne's detractors. What is oddest in his stricture is not the charge of "complete neglect of the poetic quality of the plays"[116] or even the "overstated, certainly useless, paragraphs of rhetorical and amateurish praise."[117] Most surprising is the neglect of Swinburne's credo: "It is not, so to speak, the literal but the spiritual order which I have studied to observe and to indicate: the periods which I seek to define belong not to chronology but to art."[118] If Knight adopted his restructuring of time from Swinburne, he has added to it a second element not at all to Swinburne's liking. The trick of allegory, so much a part of Knight's work, is generally attributed to the Victorian critics. Dowden, as we saw, indulged in it to some extent. Gervinus did to a much greater extent. Swinburne correctly recognized that both the tendency to allegorize and the technique of rigid scientific verse tests were the product of German scholarship carried to excess: the one conjectural beyond all evidence, the other minute and rigid to absurdity. (This fine sense of proportion is astonishing in view of Swinburne's mental illness and subsequent breakdown.) Most of his energy was directed against misuse of the new scientific apparatus. Of critics who saw Shakespeare's plays as systems of sym-

[116] "As the technical work of a painter appeals to the eye, so the technical work of a poet appeals to the ear. It follows that men who have none are as likely to arrive at any profitable end by the application of metrical tests to the work of Shakespeare as a blind man by the application of his theory of colours to the work of Titian." (*Study of Shakespeare*, p. 4.)

[117] *Sovereign Flower*, p. 287.

[118] *Study of Shakespeare*, p. 16.

bol, Swinburne wrote: "Others fell becalmed offshore in a German fog of philosophic theories, and would not be persuaded that the house of words they had built in honour of Shakespeare was 'dark as hell,' seeing 'it had bay windows transparent as barricadoes, and the clear-stories towards the south-north were as lustrous as ebony.' "[119] Notwithstanding Swinburne, allegorizing is still construed as a Victorian vice. In his introduction to the Arden *Tempest*, Frank Kermode says of Knight:

> It is not his fault if we do not see that certain romance-themes acquired special values for Shakespeare before he wrote *The Tempest*—that, for instance, the equation sea=fortune, long implicit, becomes emphatic in *Pericles* and *The Tempest*; that there is a special significance in the habit of treating voyages as "all but suicidal"; in the association of children, and birth, with tempests; in the symbolism of feasts, especially broken feasts (*Macbeth, Timon, Tempest*); in the myth of gentleness and royal blood; in the tempest-music complex as finally expressed in Prospero's dismissal of the spirits; and in the constant reiteration in *The Tempest* of themes earlier explored in the tragedies.[120]

Without entering into the validity of Knight's interpretation, this is allegorizing of the kind Swinburne loathed. And Kermode's next sentence clearly indicates that he thinks the procedure is characteristically nineteenth century: "We may complain that the last attempt occasionally sinks to the level of that kind of allegorical interpretation Dr Knight made obsolete. . . ."—presumably in his annihilation of windy Victorian critics like Swinburne.

We have followed in some detail the New Shakspere Society from Furnivall's brave credo of 1874 to the disreputable and abusive pamphlet of 1881 *The "Co." of Pigsbrook and Co.* I have done this not to catalogue the literary infighting of the 1870's and 1880's but because at heart the Swinburne-Furnivall controversy

[119] *Study of Shakespeare*, p. 3.
[120] Frank Kermode, ed., *The Tempest*, Arden Edition, pp. lxxxiv–lxxxv.

was never resolved. Here as elsewhere we still cope with a problem first articulated in the Victorian era. We seem to be closer to a solution by virtue of what we can learn from their experience. Scientific and aesthetic critics confront one another today no more decorously than did Swinburne and Furnivall nearly a century ago. Swinburne's aestheticism, along with his outraged virulence, has been inherited by F. R. Leavis, whereas C. P. Snow, with far greater restraint, has taken the scientific position articulated by Furnivall. Since the conflict of the two cultures is still raging, it might be better to go back to the 1930's and see the Furnivall-Swinburne position taken up by John Dover Wilson and L. C. Knights (the latter himself an editor of *Scrutiny*). I cite Knights' *Explorations* because so much of it is pure gold and because these essays, I think, will take their place as a permanent addition to our understanding of Shakespeare—this despite glaring misstatements about things Victorian. Knights says, for example:

> That century [the nineteenth] saw the emergence of the Shake-spearean, uncontaminated, as often as not, by any interest outside the Elizabethan field—a phenomenon which Dryden and John-son—or even Kames and Richardson—would have found it hard to understand. Criticism was not only more and more closely as-sociated with scholarship (which might have been all to the good) but dependent upon and subsidiary to it—a reversal of rôles which is responsible for the dismal spate of academic theses under which we suffer. (The thesis, it is worth remarking, is the key to a uni-versity teaching post.) Shakespeare scholarship progressed by *accumulation* rather than by a process of growth or development from a centre. It became a heavy industry, and to-day it has its monopolies and trusts, its extraordinarily efficient higher person-nel, its shock-troopers and its navvies.[121]

Organization, of course, is a characteristic of the nineteenth cen-tury, but as for the "uncontaminated" specialist, a reader of this history can only look back at the principal contributors. Abbott reorganized the City of London School, wrote science fiction along-side religious novels, and later became a proficient student of early Christianity. Almost everyone—certainly Furnivall, who most nearly fits the role of organization man—was vitally committed to his century, and tried to relate Shakespeare to the problems of the Victorian age. A. W. Ward, who became master of Peterhouse, seems to have been as busy a man as C. P. Snow. The index to Swinburne's letters covers almost every topic significant to the second half of the nineteenth century.

Fortunately, asides like this do not damage Knights' thesis; they are peripheral and almost obiter dicta. Further along in that same essay, "Shakespeare and Shakespeareans," Knights reviews one of the principal achievements of the new scientific bibliography, Wilson's edition of *Hamlet* and his two important volumes of commentary.[122] The claims made for scientific research, although stated in this instance by an unfriendly source, bring us back to the 1870's:

> The bibliographical method employed by Dr. Wilson—if method is the word for a process which, in spite of explicit disclaimers, is tending to become an end in itself in Shakespearean circles—is very far removed from the hit or miss eclecticism of editors in "the pre-Pollardian era." Indeed the prestige which the new bibliography at present enjoys is largely due to the impression that it is able to convey of being an exact science, by means of which we can hope to approach "certainty" concerning what Shakespeare wrote, or intended to write.[123]

Wilson's apparatus is very different from Fleay's, but he shows considerable confidence in altering the text of *Hamlet* according to the scientific laws he himself has helped determine. As Swinburne

[121] L. C. Knights, *Explorations: Essays in Criticism Mainly on the Literature of the Seventeenth Century*, pp. 94–95.

[122] *Hamlet*, ed. J. Dover Wilson. J. Dover Wilson, *The Manuscript of Shakespeare's Hamlet and the Problems of Its Transmission* (1934).

[123] Knights, *Explorations*, p. 102.

had observed, "the narrow and slippery reef of verbal emendation" is one upon which "our native pilots were too many of them prone to steer."[124] Knights, like Swinburne, is indignant, and, after summarizing Wilson's theory of transmission, proceeds to particulars:

> It seems best to take a particular example. In Chapter I, Dr. Wilson quotes three lines from Claudius's speech at the beginning of Act III, scene iii, which run, according to Q2,
>
> > The termes of our estate may not endure
> > Hazerd so neer's as doth hourely grow
> > Out of his browes
>
> —"which is on the face of it absurd." The Folio has "dangerous" instead of "neer's" and "lunacies" instead of "browes." Most modern editors reject "dangerous"—an obvious tautology—and accept "lunacies," but, says Dr. Wilson, they "do not enquire whether the readings in the variant pairs . . . may not be textually so closely knit that no editor should put them asunder."[125]

Knights fairly reproduces Wilson's chain of reasoning and concludes:

> The upshot is . . . that Dr. Wilson decides to read "brawls"— "which would make 'browes' a combined $a{:}o$ and $l{:}e$ error, that is to say, nothing at all out of the way"—and common sense and bibliographical principles are alike vindicated.[126]

Knights next proceeds to demonstrate what is wrong with verbal emendation. Significantly, he does it without recourse to Wilson's scientific bibliography. Knights' criteria operate in a wholly different field of reality—not better, one should add, or worse, but different, like those lines in solid geometry which never intersect. Knights proceeds:

---

[124] *A Study of Shakespeare*, p. 3. Edwards noticed a great deal of this in Warburton's edition of Shakespeare (1747) (*Canons of Criticism*, pp. 19–22).

[125] Knights, *Explorations*, p. 103.

[126] Knights, *Explorations*, p. 104.

I have quoted the one passage at length not merely because it is a good example of the way in which Dr. Wilson goes to work. "Browes" is *not* a nonsense word. Presumably Hamlet had spent a good part of the play scene staring at the King, and "hazerd" may as well "grow out of his browes" as Banquo may "grow" and "harvest" in Duncan's bosom, or a sorrow be "rooted" in the memory. Moreover there is a particular appropriateness in the conjunction of "browes" (face-eyes-mind) with the organic suggestion of "grow": Hamlet is a continually hostile force, and it is of this that the King is thinking rather than of a particular exhibition of hostility. The bibliographical machinery has merely worked in the direction decided by the taste of the editor.[127]

Because of the enormous prestige now enjoyed by the word "science"—far greater than in Furnivall's day—what Knights says next is very important:

> There is no need to collect instances where Dr. Wilson has plumped for a reading on the grounds that it is "completely and convincingly Shakespearean," and *then* brought the machinery to bear, since he is himself explicit: "It is true, as I have all along made clear . . . that the final arbiter in any particular textual decision must be the judgment and taste of the editor who makes it. . . . Yet [through the development of the new bibliographical methods] a definite corner has been turned." It seems to me a very indefinite corner.[128]

Indefinite or not, scientific bibliography has grown mightily in the

[127] Knights, *Explorations*, p. 104. Knights has centered on an important example because Greg, who often disagreed with Wilson, concurs that "browes" "is impossible, and we may suppose that it is just because it is impossible that the folio started guessing, but we are bound to do our best with it. Mr. Dover Wilson suggests a misreading of 'brawls.' I do not know whether his conjecture is right, but I am sure that his method is sound." W. W. Greg, "Principles of Emendation in Shakespeare," in Ridler, ed., *Shakespeare Criticism 1919–1935*, p. 106.

[128] Knights, *Explorations*, p. 104. The New Arden *Hamlet* has not yet appeared and it will be interesting to see how the editor, Harold Jenkins, treats this problem.

past thirty years, and it is important to remember the subjective nature or at least the subjective elements in bibliographical law however we choose to assess the law's validity.

John Dover Wilson had not yet completed his Cambridge Edition (*The Poems* and *The Sonnets* did not appear until 1966) before still newer schools of scientific criticism once again illustrated the revolution eating its own children. In his lectures on bibliography, delivered in 1959 and published in 1964 as *Bibliography and Textual Criticism*, Fredson Bowers is very hard on Wilson, but he makes no mention of Knights, nor does he discuss this particular crux from the point of view of the newest bibliography. Looking back to the 1930's, he writes: "From our present point of experience, for instance, it is genuinely sad to look back to the high confidence of a John Dover Wilson juggling the bolts of the New Bibliography like the hero of a Strauss tone poem."[129]

A love of literature—the relation of books to imaginative life—is so much baggage to the scientific critic. In his world, "a sound classical education and a First in Greats seem to have little pertinence."[130] I do not see how anyone with a love of literature can be happy with the state of affairs Bowers describes. It is cause for lamentation that for the past quarter century advances in Shakespeare studies have been carried out not by humanists but, rather, by scientific bibliographers. The danger, I think, is that even Shakespeare is falling into the hands of men who need have no love of literature. An IBM or Xerox scientist on loan to a university and quite indifferent to the university as a repository of learning and tradition, may define the scope of Shakespeare's message. This, it seems to me, is dangerous, but not to Bowers: "One cannot repeat too often that when the evidence of analytical bibliography can be made available, literary and historical judgment must be limited

129 Fredson Bowers, *Bibliography and Textual Criticism*, p. 3.
130 Bowers, p. 5.

by bibliographical probabilities and must never run contrary to mechanical findings."[131]

I do not think that aesthetic and scientific criticism can ever be brought into complete harmony. As each of our eyes sees separate images, which are then coordinated, the scientific critic sees a work of art different from the humanist, and this division is apparent throughout *Explorations*. In criticizing the new Cambridge scientists in the person of John Dover Wilson,[132] Knights seems to believe in historical necessity and some form of the Marxian ethic. Leavis and Snow seem to have much more in common than their acrimonious controversy indicates. This interpenetration of positions is not surprising when we look back to Furnivall as a Victorian humanist; then too, Swinburne's acceptance of science runs throughout his correspondence. We can now see the Swinburne-Furnivall controversy as one aspect of the Victorian failure to mesh the arts with science. A new synthesis is surely the latest plea of C. P. Snow in this century-old dispute.

In narrowing the controversy to our own field of literary inquiry, one distinction between art and the sciences should be stressed. Here, unlike in most fields, it is the scientists who look backward whereas the humanists are progressive. These adjectives are meant to be descriptive, nothing more, but the scientists necessarily work back toward antiquity whereas the humanists are concerned with today. Scientific criticism tells us what words Shakespeare actually used, what those words meant to his audience, and what underlying ideas they presupposed. This applies to scientists from the New Shakspere Society to John Dover Wilson and

---

[131] Bowers, p. 29.

[132] Swinburne recognized Cambridge as the seat of "scientific" inquiry in the 1870's: "Have not certain wise men of the east of England—Cantabrigian Magi, led by the star of their goddess Mathesis . . .—have they not detected in the very heart of this tragedy [*Macbeth*] the 'paddling palms and pinching fingers' of Thomas Middleton?" (*A Study of Shakespeare*, p. 183).

Fredson Bowers. The underlying humanist question is always: "What does Shakespeare mean today? What has he to say relevant to my own condition?" Again, Knights expresses the humanist credo, this time in the conclusion to *Some Shakespearean Themes*:

> The argument of this extended essay—which obviously makes no pretence to inclusiveness or finality—is, I trust, sufficiently clear. What I have tried to suggest is a point of view from which Shakespeare's plays can be seen as related parts of a continuous exploration of the reality that is common to all men. . . . It is the strength, integrity and coherence . . . of his *poetic thought*, that makes his work something properly described as a philosophic achievement, though of a kind that could only be made by a poet. He is concerned not with the speculation about the ultimate nature of things, the relation of mind to matter, and so on, but with the question of value as it can be known and embodied under the conditions of life as we know it![133]

But for Knights of course, knowing the conditions of life presupposes a knowledge of science, particularly social science. Knights' own plea for the integration of science with art occupies the final chapter of *Explorations*, called "The University Teaching of English and History: A Plea for Correlation." It appeared first in 1939, but seems entirely appropriate to conditions in the 1960's. For "history," one must of course read "science," and "English" in his title is shorthand for the humanities.

It would seem that these two forms of apprehending reality will always remain in conflict and that our job is to be continuously aware of the differences governing the underlying assumption about any given work of art. With this difference in mind, perhaps in time the two disciplines can be made to function with that same closeness of mesh and enrichment of perspective we associate with human vision.

An early, abortive step in that direction was taken by the Vic-

[133] L. C. Knights, *Some Shakespearean Themes*, pp. 157–58.

torians whose history has been represented here. But not everything written in the twentieth century derives from the nineteenth. Surely, we are not reduced to the role of Esau begging a crumb of blessing. There are restrictions implicit within the Victorian vision —blind spots and simple lacunae.

AESTHETICS AND MORALITY are more closely interrelated than many wish to acknowledge: they are inseparables.

—Pauline Kael

The three great impulses of Keats' nature were "Verse, Fame, and Beauty." Shelley wished to work upon people by his poetry to shape them to his own way. Keats pursued beauty for its own sake, content to have it exist of itself in the world, and by his act in poetry.

This is the poet of pure poetry, not one using the medium as a means to another end.

—Edmund Fuller reviewing *John Keats: The Making of a Poet* by Aileen Ward

If anyone were asked to describe what it is which distinguishes the writings of a man of genius who is also a great man of the world from all other writings, I think he would use these . . . words, "animated moderation." . . . The best and almost perfect instance of this in English is Scott. Homer was perfect in it, as far as we can judge; Shakespeare is often perfect in it for long together, though then, from the defects of a bad education and a vicious age, all at once he loses himself in excesses.

—Walter Bagehot, *Physics and Politics*, 1869

the limiting factor

IN THE 1930's, when critics were more confident, William Empson published *Some Versions of Pastoral*.[1] A confidence not at all misplaced and his second chapter, "Double Plots," suggests a principal lack in Victorian Shakespeare criticism. The first twenty pages or so of this essay deal with Shakespeare, but only once does he refer to a Victorian: "Swinburne said of *The Changeling* that 'the underplot from which it most absurdly and unluckily derives its title is very stupid, rather coarse, and almost vulgar,' after which it is no use saying, as he does, that it is Middleton and Rowley's greatest play, 'a work which should suffice to make either name immortal'; the thing might have good passages but would be a bad play."[2] It is Empson's chosen task to emphasize the significance of the underplot, and throughout this essay he assumes that no one has yet recognized its importance. His first paragraph concludes on a note of discovery: ". . . one might almost say that the English drama did not outlive the double plot. The matter is not only of theoretical interest; it seems likely that the double plot needs to be revived and must first be understood."[3] One hardly expects Empson to have been aware of the New Shakspere Society and its many papers devoted to double plots in English, German, or the classics. Moulton's *Shakespeare as a Dramatic Artist* had probably been forgotten,[4] but surely every Cambridge undergraduate read Bradley. Of *Lear*, Bradley writes: "By the side of Lear, his daughters, Kent,

---

[1] Empson, *Some Versions of Pastoral*.
[2] Empson, p. 46.   [3] Empson, pp. 25–26.
[4] Moulton's Chapter X is called "How Climax Meets Climax in the Centre

and the Fool, who are the principal figures in the main plot, stand Gloster and his two sons, the chief persons of the secondary plot. Now by means of this double action Shakespeare secured certain results highly advantageous even from the strictly dramatic point of view, and easy to perceive."[5] And it would not even have been necessary to read Bradley himself, since this passage is indexed under "Double action in King Lear."

But since Empson is so well read, the explanation must lie elsewhere, probably in the quotation from Bradley just cited. In the first paragraph of his Introduction, Bradley speaks of those ordinary men with "native strength and justice of perception" who read Shakespeare with greatest intensity. "Such lovers read a play more or less as if they were actors who had to study all the parts,"[6] but not for presentation on the stage. When Bradley writes that "Shakespeare secured certain results highly advantageous *even* from the strictly dramatic point of view,"[7] he is exposing a great weakness of Victorian Shakespeare criticism. The criticism is simply not dramatic. This perhaps accounts for Empson's having overlooked Victorian research into double plots and also the modern tendency to credit him with the first exploration of underplotting. The Victorians were the last print-oriented generation before the electronic innovations in communications restored the importance

---

of 'Lear.' " He observes, in part: ". . . as the main and underplot go on working side by side, they are at every turn by their antithesis throwing up one another's effect; the contrast is like the reversing of the original subject in a musical fugue" (p. 207). The third and most complete edition of Moulton's *Shakespeare as a Dramatic Artist* was published in 1906, the year of Empson's birth, whereas Bradley died in 1935, the year *Some Versions of Pastoral* first appeared.

[5] A. C. Bradley, *Shakespearean Tragedy*, pp. 205–206. Dowden, whose importance Bradley had acknowledged, devotes a paragraph to the subject. And even he (writing in 1874) does not take credit for an original insight: "Of the secondary plot of this tragedy—the story of Gloucester and his sons—Schlegel has explained one chief significance." (Dowden, *Shakspere*, pp. 235–36).

[6] Bradley, *Shakespearean Tragedy*, page 13.

[7] Bradley, pp. 205–206. Italics are mine.

of seeing and hearing via movies and the phonograph—hence, a lack of respect for the stage and a misunderstanding of the more fluid, oral tradition in Elizabethan culture.

Bernard Shaw, who as a young man had contributed papers to Furnivall's New Shakspere Society, very clearly indicates the difference between theater criticism and what the nineteenth century took to be dramatic criticism:

> "For stage purposes," wrote Shaw, "there are not many types of character available; and all the playwrights use them over and over again. Idiosyncracies are useful on the stage only to give an air of infinite variety to the standard types. Shakespear's crude Gratiano is Benedick, Berowne, and Mercutio, finally evolving through Jacques into Hamlet. He is also my Smilash, my Philanderer, my John Tanner. Take Falstaff's discourse on honor; and how far are you from Alfred Doolittle's disquisition on middle-class morality?"[8]

Nothing written by the Victorian critics displays the same sense of dramatic handling, of character as stuff to be shaped for the two hours' traffic of the stage.

It would be logically satisfying to suppose that Victorian Shakespeare productions were undramatic, and there is support for this argument. Robert Langbaum thinks that the nineteenth century saw the emergence of the dramatic monologue and simultaneous decline of dramatic conflict. This coincides with the emphasis on character, which spanned the century from Coleridge through Bradley. As it relates to Shakespeare, Langbaum's argument is summarized in Chapter V of *The Poetry of Experience*, entitled "Character versus Action in Shakespeare":

> ... the misinterpretation of Shakespeare in the nineteenth century is worth reviewing. ... They [the Victorians] read him not as

[8] Quoted in Martin Meisel, *Shaw and the Nineteenth-Century Theater*, pp. 18–19.

drama in the traditional Aristotelian sense, not in other words as a literature of external action in which the events derive meaning from their relation to a publicly acknowledged morality, but as literature of experience, in which the events have meaning inasmuch as they provide the central character with an occasion for experience—for self-expression and self-discovery. . . .

Thus, the nineteenth-century reading of Shakespeare gives great weight to the soliloquies, which are just the moments when the point of view of the central character seems to obliterate the general perspective of the play.[9]

Langbaum refers to neither Shaw nor Empson, but his book on the dramatic monologue would confirm the barrenness of nineteenth-century theater. Unfortunately, Shaw thought that the Victorian repertory companies maintained a rich and vigorous tradition of Shakespeare interpretation: "Of the English speaking stars incomparably the greatest was Barry Sullivan [1824–91], who was in his prime when I was in my teens, the last of the race of heroic figures which had dominated the stage since the palmy Siddons-Kemble days. . . ."[10] And he felt that nineteenth-century interpretation was impressive enough to inspire great original drama. For Shaw, the failure to create these plays rests not with the actors or their interpretation but, as might be expected, within the economic system. Meisel agrees with Shaw, and I cite both arguments as he links them together:

Looking back with considerable historical acumen, Shaw felt that a century of actors like Kean, Macready, Barry Sullivan, and Irving ought to have inspired a group of monumental heroic plays, "comparable in intensity to those of Aeschylus, Sophocles, and Euripides"; but instead: "Sheridan Knowles, Bulwer Lytton, Wills, and Tennyson produced a few glaringly artificial high horses for the great actors of their time; but the playwrights

[9] Robert Langbaum, *The Poetry of Experience*, p. 160.
[10] Quoted in Meisel, pp. 13–14.

proper, who really kept the theatre going, and were kept going by the theatre, did not cater for the great actors: they could not afford to compete with a bard who was not of an age but for all time, and who had, moreover, the overwhelming attraction for the actor-managers of not charging author's fees."[11]

At all events, the best criticism of Shakespeare was not dramatic, and it would be helpful to be able to find an explanation in the non-dramatic quality of nineteenth-century acting. The only critic whose dramatic sense Shaw acknowledged was G. H. Lewes (himself a playwright) whom Shaw called "the most able and brilliant critic between Hazlitt and our own contemporaries."[12] Shaw is talking about *On Actors and the Art of Acting* (1875), but Lewes has very little to say about Shakespeare in his chapter "Shakespeare as Actor and Critic" beyond the self-revealing surmise that he was probably indifferent to the stage.

The general interest in character at the expense of action culminated, I think, in Virginia Woolf. Leslie Stephen's essay "Shakespeare as a Man" (1901) is one illustration of this interest narrowed to the field of Shakespeare studies. Bagehot's "Shakespeare —The Man" (1853), yet an earlier example of the genre, is worth examining for the crimp this method imposed on Shakespeare studies. (Against these frankly biographical studies, the wrath of *Scrutiny* might most profitably have been directed. Bradley never asks how many children Lady Macbeth had unless the question is relevant to the life of the play.)

Walter Bagehot is probably the only important literary figure whose complete works were published by an insurance company, and this oddity defines much of his criticism.[13] More than any other of the men considered in this history, he refutes L. C. Knights'

[11] Meisel, p. 84.
[12] Meisel, p. 35 n., 34.
[13] *The Works of Walter Bagehot*, first published by the Travelers Insurance Company.

charge that the Victorians were cloistered academicians. Here is Bagehot, a nonconformist London University man, on the virtues of an Oxford education:

No one can deny to it very great and very peculiar merits: but certainly it is not an exciting place, and its education operates as a narcotic rather than as a stimulant. Most of its students devote their lives to a single profession, and we may observe among them a kind of sacred torpidity. In many rural parsonages there are men of very great cultivation, who are sedulous in their routine duties, who attend minutely to the ecclesiastical state of the souls in their village, but who are perfectly devoid of general intellectual interests.[14]

Bagehot's essay "Shakespeare—the Man" is relatively early (1853), although most of his literary work belongs to the 1850's. His father-in-law died in 1860, and thereafter Bagehot was pre-occupied with the more weighty affairs of the *Economist*. Still, the essay was enormously popular throughout the century, and S. S. McClure brought the essay out for American readers as a separate publication in 1901. The title alone indicates that Bagehot's interest is nondramatic, nor can we look for the extreme sensitivity Bradley was to bring to character analysis. If Coleridge saw Hamlet created in his image, for Bagehot, Shakespeare was a man much like himself. Like Bagehot, Shakespeare enjoyed the hunt, and he quotes the stanzas about poor Wat from *Venus and Adonis* to prove his point: "It is absurd, by the way, to say we know *nothing* about the man who wrote that: we know that he had been after a hare. It is idle to allege that mere imagination would tell him that a hare is apt to run among a flock of sheep, or that its so doing disconcerts the scent of hounds. But no single citation really represents the power of the argument."[15] An experienced sportsman, Bagehot

---

[14] "Mr. Gladstone," in *Works*, III, 91–92. First published in *National Review*, July, 1860, and then reprinted in *Biographical Studies*, ed. Richard Holt Hutton.
[15] *Works*, I, 259.

concludes with a banking image borrowed from Johnson, that the richness of allusion employed here by Shakespeare is beyond the range of mere imagination: "A man who knows little of nature may write one excellent delineation, as a poor man may have one bright guinea; real opulence consists in having many. What truly indicates excellent knowledge is the habit of constant, sudden, and almost unconscious allusion, which implies familiarity. . . ."[16] Shakespeare is conservative like Bagehot himself, who went from the management of his mother's banking interest in Somerset to his father-in-law's London *Economist*. And if like Keats's Shakespeare, Bagehot too led a life of allegory, not much is made of it—the point is embedded in the middle of a paragraph: "We see but one aspect of our neighbour, as we see but one side of the moon; in either case there is also a dark half, which is unknown to us. We all come down to dinner, but each has a room to himself."[17] Bagehot concludes his essay on a note which must have delighted the readers of the *Economist*:

> We see generally, indeed, in Shakespeare's works, the popular author, the successful dramatist: there is a life and play in his writings rarely to be found except in those who have had habitual good luck; and who, by the tact of experience, feel the minds of their readers at every word, as a good rider feels the mouth of his horse. But it would have been difficult quite to make out whether the profits so accruing had been profitably invested,—whether the genius to create such illusions was accompanied with the care and judgment necessary to put out their proceeds properly in actual life. . . . The reverential nature of Englishmen has carefully preserved what they thought the great excellence of their poet,—that he made a fortune.[18]

[16] *Works*, I, 259.
[17] *Works*, I, 280.
[18] *Works*, I, 301. Bagehot's essay is the high-water mark of Victorian materialism. Dowden, writing twenty years later, is much less emphatic concerning the advantages of wealth.

Whatever reservations Bagehot has about Shakespeare concern the nervous intensity of his style: throughout his essays Bagehot reverts to the stricture by Matthew Arnold quoted at the beginning of my second chapter.

Nor is Bagehot any better in that other field of Victorian scholarship—historical inquiry. The ostensible purpose of this essay was the review of two recent Shakespeare texts, one by Guizot (of no importance); the other, John Payne Collier's infamous *Notes and Emendations to the Text of Shakespeare's Plays* (1853). This forgery, promptly attacked by Samuel Weller Singer in *The Text of Shakespeare Vindicated from the Interpolations and Corruptions Advocated by John Payne Collier Esq. in His Notes and Emendations*,[19] brought about the collapse of the first Shakespeare Society. These supposed corrections which Collier claimed he discovered in a copy of the Second Folio were exposed by N. E. S. A. Hamilton of the British Museum in 1859. But Singer, whose book was also published in 1853, and might well have been reviewed by Bagehot in his essay, suggested as much in his Preface:

> The following pages will however clearly demonstrate how very far from probable, or even possible, it is that the correctors of this volume had any ancient authority for their doings; that, on the contrary, the greater part of them are adopted from recent annotators; and that, of what are original, or can be considered new readings, abundance are changes for the worse, and a still larger number entirely unnecessary and impertinent![20]

Singer is indignant at Collier's "emendations," but Bagehot is only bored. Referring to Collier only once, Bagehot remarks that "It is difficult to fancy Shakespeare perusing a volume of such annotations, though we allow that we admire them ourselves."[21] Admire

[19] London, 1853.
[20] Singer, pp. xi–xii. Halliwell-Phillipps' *Life of William Shakespeare* had incorporated a large number of Collier's fabrications—a suspiciously large number.

them he may, but Bagehot shows no interest in either the skill with which Collier interpolates his forgeries or the malicious delight of Singer in uncovering them. If Bagehot was uninterested in scholarship, there were other Victorians to make up his lack. The most serious shortcoming of Victorian Shakespeare study is the scanting of Coleridge and the imagination.

Empson thought he had rediscovered the double plot, and we have indicated that he was wrong.[22] His tutor I. A. Richards had charged a few years earlier (in 1925) that Coleridge's distinction between Fancy and Imagination and, indeed, the whole concept of imagination had been ignored by his predecessors.[23] Richards, it seems to me, is quite right in reverting so consistently to Coleridge in his *Principles of Literary Criticism*,[24] but he has no explanation as to why Coleridge was so ignored:

> *Biographia Literaria*, Ch. XIII. "The primary IMAGINA-TION I hold to be the living Power and prime Agent of all human perception, and as a repetition in the finite mind of the eternal act of creation in the infinite I AM." The luminous hints dropped by Coleridge in the neighbourhood of this sentence would seem to have dazzled succeeding speculators. How otherwise explain why they have been overlooked.[25]

In his chapter entitled "The Imagination," Richards adds: "The

[21] Bagehot, *Works*, I, 298.

[22] Except of course in a dramatic, as distinct from a literary, sense—that distinction has been the gravamen of this chapter.

[23] Coleridge on Imagination can be found in Dugald Stewart's very popular *Philosophical Essays* (Edinburgh, 1810), Part II, Essay Fourth, page 506, where Stewart asserts "*creative* imagination . . . forms the chief element in poetical genius." When "the Power of Imagination" is alive, "the mind awakening, as if from a trance, to a new existence, becomes habituated to the most interesting aspects of life and of nature; the intellectual eye is 'purged of its film'; and things the most familiar and unnoticed, disclose charms invisible before." (p. 509)

[24] I. A. Richards, *Principles of Literary Criticism*.

[25] Richards, *Principles of Literary Criticism*, p. 191 n.

original formulation was Coleridge's greatest contribution to critical theory, and except in the way of interpretation, it is hard to add anything to what he has said, though ... some things may be taken away from it with advantage."[26] It is more than forty years since Richards' book appeared, and nobody will quarrel with his assessment of Coleridge's contribution to the workings of the poetic mind and his sorting out of metaphor from mere simile. It is the great lack in Victorian criticism.

But Richards' own explanation was probably facetious. Coleridge, it is true, said so much so badly that contemporaries overlooked the greatness of his contribution. Carlyle's scathing references to him in *The Life of John Sterling*, published in 1851, provide a gauge to contemporary opinion. Alba H. Warren says "Coleridge now so completely covers the critical horizon of the nineteenth century that it is easy to forget he came into his reputation late. German criticism counted directly with individual critics such as Carlyle and Dallas, but more generally it operated through Wordsworth's treatment of the imagination as that generated further elaborations in the native tradition."[27] Bagehot knows of the distinction Coleridge made between Fancy and Imagination, but refers to it in such a way as to indicate the truth of Richards' charge that it was simply not understood. Bagehot employs the concept as an incidental metaphor and never relates it to Shakespeare's art:

> In early youth it is perhaps not true that the passions, taken generally, are particularly violent, or that the imagination is in any remarkable degree powerful; but it is certain that the fancy (which, though it be in the last resort but a weak stroke of that same faculty which when it strikes hard we call imagination, may yet for this purpose be looked on as distinct) is particularly wake-

[26] Richards, *Principles of Literary Criticism*, p. 242.
[27] Alba H. Warren, *English Poetic Theory 1825–1865*, p. 210.

ful, and that the gentler species of passions are more absurd than they are afterwards.[28]

When Bagehot quotes *Venus and Adonis*, it is to prove that Shakespeare must have been a sportsman. He does not even mention that Coleridge's illustrations of the difference between Fancy and Imagination came from this poem.

To answer Richards' question and to explain why Coleridge was overlooked, it may be necessary to do no more than revert to some great truths articulated in Johnson's Preface of 1765: "The chief desire of him that comments an author is to show how much other commentators have corrupted and obscured him. The opinions prevalent in one age as truths above the reach of controversy are confuted and rejected in another and rise again to reception in remoter times. Thus the human mind is kept in motion without progress."[29] The disorganization with which Coleridge presented his material contributed of course to his neglect, and no one can say how long he may have remained obscure. But his rediscovery and growing importance are related, I think, to the discoveries and theories of that Continental Victorian Sigmund Freud, who provided the machinery for the full analysis of imagery and the relation of random associations so characteristic of Coleridge. It was only a matter of time until some literary man who had been drawn to psychoanalysis happened on Coleridge and reinterpreted him in the light of the new science.[30]

Coleridge's distinction between Fancy and Imagination, as reinterpreted in the twentieth century, is responsible for much fine modern criticism. F. E. Halliday, I have suggested, tends to skimp

---

[28] Bagehot, *Works*, I, 285.

[29] W. K. Wimsatt, Jr., ed., *Samuel Johnson on Shakespeare*, p. 57.

[30] It is no coincidence that the first preliminary page of *The Meaning of Meaning* by C. K. Ogden and I. A. Richards (1930), first published in 1923, lists dozens of publications of the International Library of Psychology, Philosophy and Scientific Method, and that the general editor was C. K. Ogden.

the Victorians. But he is very good on Shakespeare's poetry. The reason, I think, goes back to Coleridge. In *The Poetry of Shakespeare's Plays*,[31] written for the "ordinary" lover of Shakespeare, Halliday takes Coleridge's insight, adds to it what has become coin in our own century about the workings of the imagination, and writes a very good book about the growth of Shakespeare's art.[32] A straightforward paragraph like the following is not to be found in nineteenth-century criticism. Halliday is discussing the change that overtook Shakespeare about the time he was writing *Henry IV*:

> The action is no longer subordinated to the imagery, but imagery is subdued to the action, and metaphor, stripped of its elaborations, assumes a new form. In the early poetry, in which the line is so emphatically the unit, a favourite form of short metaphor is that of a noun followed by a prepositional phrase:
>> The coward conquest of a wretch's knife.
>> The barren tender of a poet's debt.
>> And shake the yoke of inauspicious stars. . . .
>
> And then there is the metaphor contained in paired nouns:
>> Who is sweet Fortune's minion and her pride.
> This is a variation of the old form, in which it might occur as "the treasur'd minion of sweet Fortune," but Shakespeare preferred to combine the old and sonorous form of noun-prepositional phrase with the new device of paired words, and by a simple reversal created the type of metaphor that becomes almost a hallmark of his middle style. In this new idiom, "sweet Fortune's minion and her pride" would read "the pride and minion of sweet Fortune," and thus we have in I *Henry IV*:
>> For the hot vengeance and the rod of heaven.
>> The very bottom and the soul of hope.
>> The quality and hair of our attempt. . . .
>
> . . . typically, one is monosyllabic, concrete and Saxon, the other

[31] London, 1954.
[32] His idea of growth in time is of course Victorian.

polysyllabic, abstract and Latin in origin, as *rod-vengeance, hair-quality*.[33]

There is nothing really original in the foregoing; in fact, these paragraphs represent the common run of contemporary critical opinion, and I have quoted them for that reason. Ifor Evans covers much the same ground in *The Language of Shakespeare's Plays*.[34] But all these studies of differentiation in imagery grow out of Coleridge, and close analysis of a poet's word images spills over into the poetry too. It sounds like a commonplace, but one has only to think back to Swinburne and see that this is not so. Swinburne's *Study of Shakespeare* refers to Shakespeare's poetry on every third page. He justly prides himself on his own fine ear, and contrasts his sense for poetry with that of the grubby statisticians affiliated with the New Shakspere Society. But not once does he tell us of what poetry consists. Admittedly, Coleridge's "best words in the best order" is not wholly satisfactory, but there is no comparison between the looseness of Swinburne on his own ground and Halliday's discussing Prospero's "Our revels now are ended." Let me quote part of Halliday's analysis to demonstrate from what a strong base criticism can now proceed:

> In these lines [from: *Our revels now are ended* to: *Is rounded with the sleep*], perhaps the most beautiful that Shakespeare ever wrote, the triple counterpoint of imagery, phrase and rhythm reaches its final perfection. Though metrically almost regular, much of their beauty lies in the counter-rhythm induced by the assonantal sequences of false trochees and related words—*revels, temples; actors, fabric, pageant, baseless*—sequences that are linked by that of the verbs, *ended, melted, faded*, with their remote connotations and fading cadences.[35]

[33] Halliday, *The Poetry of Shakespeare's Plays*, pp. 40–41.
[34] London, 1952. 2d edition, 1959.
[35] Halliday, *The Poetry of Shakespeare's Plays*, p. 51.

afterword

Bᴜᴛ ᴛʜᴇ sᴇᴀ ɪs ɴoᴛ ꜰᴜʟʟ. And I should now like to suggest a direction Shakespeare criticism might profitably take. The importance of modern criticism rests in having united the psychological and imaginative insight of the romantics with the historical perspective of Malone and the Victorians. I. A. Richards did important work in rediscovering Coleridge's work on imagination. He has been important too for insisting on the value of art today for each new reader as distinct from the student of historical perspective in sociology, economics, or comparative culture. This follows from his interest in Coleridge, who operated wholly without the discipline of historical context. The importance of literature as a *magister vitae* is continually stressed by him as well as by F. R. Leavis. The most important contribution of *Scrutiny* is the unstressed assumption that literature matters, that it possesses value, and that man has some freedom to choose or discriminate from among the many insistent demands of competing disciplines. Richards expresses this necessity keenly in the final chapter of *Principles of Literary Criticism*:

> For clear and impartial awareness of the nature of the world in which we live and the development of attitudes which will enable us to live in it finely are both necessities, and neither can be subordinated to the other. They are almost independent, such connections as exist in well-organised individuals being adventitious. Those who find this a hard saying may be invited to consider the effect upon them of those works of art which most unmistakably attune them to existence. The central experience of Tragedy and

its chief value is an attitude indispensable for a fully developed life. But in the reading of *King Lear* what facts verifiable by science, or accepted and believed in as we accept and believe in ascertained facts, are relevant? None whatever.[1]

This credo leads into the philosophy of *Scrutiny*. It would be too much out of the way to trace it back to Matthew Arnold, though worth the doing—perhaps almost as valuable as Richards' rehabilitation of Coleridge. The weakness of Richards' criticism—and *Scrutiny*'s too—has been loss of historical perspective.[2] And the best analysis of Richards' "astereopsis" is appropriately Helen Gardner's *The Business of Criticism*[3]—appropriate because three of the essays incorporate the Riddell Memorial Lectures at Durham for 1956. As Miss Gardner announces in her Preface, "The terms of the Deed of Foundation for these lectures demand that the lectures should be concerned with the relation between religion and contemporary developments of thought, 'with particular emphasis on the Ethics and Tenets of Christianity.' "[4] The struggle between immediacy and historical perspective is the heritage of everyone born into a religious home, to a degree that cannot be understood from the secular environment without. For the world is ever new, but the word of revelation is rooted in antiquity. God's voice speaks with more immediacy and authority than any living father, and his message is incorporated into documents incredibly ancient. And anyone who attempts to conserve the past is forced to reconcile these conflicting positions. Miss Gardner, as a practicing Christian,

[1] I. A. Richards, *Principles of Literary Criticism*, p. 282.

[2] Generalization is difficult. L. C. Knights, a coeditor of *Scrutiny*, grounded his criticism in the historical perspective of Marxism. Richards occasionally acknowledges historical perspective, but only to discount it: "A chief modern difficulty in such understanding comes from the recent development of the historical sense. . . . This, at first sight, should make good reading easier." *How To Read A Page*, 1961, p. 13.

[3] Oxford, 1959.

[4] Gardner, Preface, p. vii.

brings to literary criticism a habit of mind she must have formulated long before there was any need to relate the immediacy of Richards or Leavis to their historical context. Interestingly, Miss Gardner is arguing away from herself—she is committed by her religious tradition to the immediacy of the Word while pleading in these pages for the perspective and mutation of the centuries. Her entire book reflects the richness of contemporary criticism, blending Coleridgean imaginative insight with the historical perspective of later-nineteenth-century investigation.

Richards, whose criticism develops almost wholly from Coleridge, comes in for sharp criticism. Miss Gardner says of the two traditions:

> All works of art, whatever else they may be, are historical objects, and to approach them as such is, I believe, a fundamental necessity if they are to realize their power fully over us. "All good art is contemporary" is a well-known critical maxim. It needs to be balanced by the statement that "All art, including contemporary art, is historical."[5]

Her next paragraph confronts those who attempt

> in this century to ignore these truisms, or to depreciate their importance. . . . This attempt to isolate the work of art and treat it as a thing *per se*, putting it under a kind of mental bell-jar, disregards the nature of art, and makes criticism a special kind of activity, divorced from our normal habits as readers. . . . Dr. I. A. Richards undertook the experiment of presenting poems "by themselves," without even an author's name attached, to classes of undergraduates, and published the results of the protocols in *Practical Criticism*. The experiment proved, I think, not the incapacity of the readers, but the futility of the method.[6]

All of what she says is so relevant to modern criticism that I am re-

[5] Gardner, p. 17.
[6] Gardner, pp. 18–19.

luctant to cut or criticize. But whatever deficiencies Richards' method entails, the suggestion of "impersonal, scientific" poetry is unfair. Anyone trying to explicate the meaning of meaning seems destined to obscurity. What happened, I think, was that the traditional moral counters broke down about the same time that national currencies became debased. As art critics find moral and aesthetic value in the shapes that have replaced the tangible figures of nineteenth-century painting, the new critic finds purpose and meaning in a new set of ethical counters. The *Wall Street Journal* reviewer writes of art for the sake of art,[7] whereas *Partisan Review* cries sternly for morality. So, for example, a *Scrutiny* reviewer might speak of the pattern of texture, or equally the texture of pattern in, say, Shakespeare's Roman plays. Either argument would lead to some ethical conclusion expressed as harmony or design if not the traditional values of good and evil.

It is, I believe, because Miss Gardner has come to terms with historical necessity—a value, I like to think, of the nineteenth century—that she can say so much in single sentences:

> Those who hold seriously to enjoyment as the true end of reading speak from within the Greek tradition which rates the life of contemplation above the life of action and holds that man's destiny is to enjoy the vision of truth, beauty, and goodness, or, to use the Christian formulation, "to glorify God and to enjoy him for ever." And the critic who, in addition, believes that the true meaning of a work of art can only be apprehended by seeing it within its historical context, but that its meaning is not limited by that context, is one who has to some degree or other parted company with Plato and does not believe that man is a soul imprisoned in a body, but that the union of soul and body make man.[8]

Within the bounds of Miss Gardner's definition, there is work for

---

[7] No matter that Edmund Fuller is misreading Keats the way some Victorians did, afraid to credit with high seriousness a writer of such intense sensuousness.

[8] Gardner, p. 21.

a generation of critics. I want only to pick up a topic at which Miss Gardner no more than hints:

> The primary critical act is a judgement, the decision that a certain piece of writing has significance and value. . . . It appeals also to my experience as a human being, to my conscience and moral life. I put the triad in this order because in literature, whose medium is words, unintelligibility prevents recognition of the presence of either beauty or wisdom. We must feel that the work "makes sense," even if at first only in patches, if we are to feel it value.[9]

With this, Richards agrees—"understanding" is one of the key words in his critical vocabulary. Indeed, more than forty years ago, when *Principles of Literary Criticism* (to which Miss Gardner alluded) first appeared, people hoped that Richards would create a scientific theory of poetry and communication. This never happened, and the reason takes us back to the nineteenth century.[10] Fleay and Swinburne were not entirely comic when they argued over the role of art and science. That Wordsworth had touched on what was to be a central topic of criticism is confirmed by the recurring appearance of this controversy. John Dover Wilson and L. C. Knights, Leavis and Snow—all represent attempts to grapple with the relation of science to literature, a problem not yet resolved but which cannot be denied.

There is a New York story about the East Side boy who made good and came back to Mother sporting his yachtsman's cap. "Look, Ma, I'm a captain!" he said. The old lady smiled wisely and answered, "By me you're a captain, by you you're a captain, but by captains, Sammy, you're no captain." More than any modern critic, Richards talks of the scientific basis on which his criticism is

---

[9] Gardner, pp. 6–7.

[10] Richards has of course come to recognize the limits of his theory: "We are likely to understand how chromosomes work long before we can give any comparable account of how a poem achieves its unity or closure." ("The Future of Poetry," in *The Screens and Other Poems*, p. 117.)

founded. There are even anatomical drawings and sketches scattered through his pages to buttress the objectivity of his thesis. But the reason he failed to create a scientific theory of criticism is that by no scientific standard, as the word is understood by biologists, chemists, or mathematicians, can his work be considered scientific. And we shall not understand how to read a page or how the written page conveys the impression of what we call poetry without an adequate theory of communication grounded in natural science.

Johnson's Preface (1765), written two hundred years after Shakespeare's birth, marveled at his vitality. Johnson affords us a superb vantage point because he is the last critic to share Shakespeare's assumption of motion without progress. Another two hundred years have since elapsed with no apparent diminution in the poet's reputation. Studies about him appear at least one a day, but we still know little concerning the mechanism which transmits his poetry from the page to the mind with such vividness. What humanists call "scientific studies" are usually bibliographical, and bibliography is one division of historical inquiry, although work with paper and chemicals brings bibliographers into closer contact with natural science than does the work of the practitioners of other literary disciplines.[11] An adequate theory of transmission from retina to occipital cortex, which must come out of the laboratory, may explain why certain Shakespearean passages still compel our absolute attention although his very words, steeped and dyed in time, no longer mean what they did one hundred years ago, let alone four hundred. We might then have an internal or Coleridgean explanation for the continuous displacement of literary values instead of the history-of-ideas studies on which we now rely. Why, for example, did Coleridge idolize Hamlet when to modern critics the prince has become an increasingly unpleasant

[11] Fleay may be excepted from this indifference to the "other culture." Born a generation or two later, he might have enjoyed a productive career investigating the natural sciences in Rutherford's Cambridge.

young man? We may be able to formulate critical positions more usefully once we know *what* Coleridge was physically responding to and how that response occurred once an impression had been received by the retina. An adequate theory of transmission might finally mediate between external historical criticism and the internal poetic or Coleridgean kind.

In the larger sense, Coleridge's approach from within was right. Very few people are interested in Elizabethan stage conventions or language by themselves, but only insofar as they help interpret the word—and, increasingly, Shakespeare provides the bread of scripture for secular generations. People are interested in Shakespeare because he has something to say today, and they are prepared to make adjustments in their own language to find out what it is. But there is a limit beyond which they cannot stretch backward in time, when the structure topples and Shakespeare becomes a foreign language. English is changing very rapidly, and how long will it be before the first paperback appears of his plays translated into modern American? But perhaps before then, through the application of scientific method, more extreme and analytic than anything Furnivall dreamed possible, we will penetrate his core of inexhaustible energy to understand why Shakespeare stood for so long, triple-brassed against the common enemy, calumniating time.

a selecteδ BIBLIOGRAPhy

Abbott, Edwin A. *Flatland: A Romance of Many Dimensions.* 2d rev. ed. London, 1884.

————. *From Letter to Spirit.* London, 1903.

————. *A Shakespearian Grammar: An Attempt to Illustrate Some of the Differences between Elizabethan and Modern English.* London, 1869.

Alexander, Peter. *Shakespeare's Henry VI and Richard III.* Cambridge, 1929.

Alumni Cantabrigiensis to 1900. Compiled by John Venn and J. A. Venn. 10 vols. Cambridge, 1922–54.

Alumni Oxonienses 1715–1886. Compiled by Joseph Foster. 4 vols. Oxford, 1887.

Arber, Edward, ed. *Transcript of the Registers of the Company of Stationers, 1554–1640.* 5 vols. London, 1875–94.

Armstrong, Edward A. *Shakespeare's Imagination.* Lincoln, Neb., 1963.

Arnold, Matthew. *The Complete Prose Works of Matthew Arnold,* ed. R. H. Super. Ann Arbor, 1960–.

Auerbach, Erich. *Mimesis.* Princeton, 1953.

Aytoun, W. E. *Firmilian.* New York, 1854.

Babbage, Charles. "On Tables of the Constants of Nature and Art," in *Annual Report of the Board of Regents of the Smithsonian Institution for 1856.* Washington, 1857, pp. 289–303.

————. *Passages from the Life of a Philosopher.* London, 1864.

Bagehot, Walter. *Physics and Politics.* Boston, 1956.

————. "Shakespeare—The Man," *Biographical Studies,* ed. Richard Holt Hutton. London, 1881.

————. *The Works of Walter Bagehot.* 5 vols. Hartford, Conn., 1889.

Bartlett, John. *A New and Complete Concordance of the Dramatic Works and Poems of Shakespeare.* New York, 1894.

Bate, Walter Jackson. *The Achievement of Samuel Johnson.* New York, 1955.

―――. *From Classic to Romantic.* Harvard, 1946.

―――. *John Keats.* Oxford, 1963.

―――. *Prefaces to Criticism.* New York, 1959.

―――. *The Stylistic Development of Keats.* New York, 1945.

Baynes, Thomas Spencer. *Shakespeare Studies.* London, 1894.

Boas, Frederick S. *Shakspere and His Predecessors.* London, 1896.

Bowden, Henry Sebastian. *The Religion of Shakespeare.* London, 1899.

Bowers, Fredson. *Bibliography and Textual Criticism.* Oxford, 1964.

―――. *On Editing Shakespeare and the Elizabethan Dramatists.* University of Pennsylvania Library, Philadelphia, 1955.

―――. *Textual and Literary Criticism.* Cambridge, 1959.

Bradley, Andrew C. *Oxford Lectures on Poetry.* 2d ed. London, 1909.

―――. *Shakespearean Tragedy.* New York, 1955.

―――. "Andrew Cecil Bradley," *Times Literary Supplement,* May 23, 1936, pp. 425–26.

Bradshaw, Henry. *Collected Papers.* Cambridge, 1889.

―――. "Henry Bradshaw," in J. Willis Clark, *Old Friends at Cambridge and Elsewhere.* London, 1900.

―――. *A Memoir of Henry Bradshaw* by G. W. Prothero. London, 1888.

Brandl, Alois. *Shakespeare and Germany.* London, 1913.

―――. "Alois Brandl," see entry under Wolfgang Keller.

Bronson, Bertrand H. *Johnson Agonistes.* Cambridge, 1946.

Brooks, Cleanth. *The Well Wrought Urn.* New York, 1947.

Brown, Charles A. *Shakespeare's Autobiographical Poems.* London, 1838.

Butler, Samuel. *Shakespeare's Sonnets.* London, 1899.

Cairncross, Andrew S., ed. *The First Part of King Henry VI.* London, 1962.

Campbell, Lily Bess. *Shakespeare's Tragic Heroes.* New York, 1960.

Carlyle, Thomas. *The Life of John Sterling.* (World's Classics). Oxford, 1907. Introduction by W. Hale White.

Cartwright, Robert. *The Footsteps of Shakspere.* London, 1862.

Chambers, Edmund K. *The Disintegration of Shakespeare.* (*Proceedings* of the British Academy, 1924–25). London, 1924.

————. *The Elizabethan Stage.* 4 vols. Oxford, 1923.

————. *Shakespeare: A Survey.* London, 1925.

————. "The Unrest in Shakespearean Studies," *The Nineteenth Century and After,* XCI (Jan.–June, 1927), 255–66.

————. *William Shakespeare: A Study of Facts and Problems.* 2 vols. Oxford, 1930.

Charlton, H. B. *Shakespearian Tragedy.* Cambridge, 1948.

Clark, G. Kitson. *The Making of Victorian England.* Cambridge, Mass., 1962.

Coleridge, Samuel Taylor. *The Notebooks of Samuel Taylor Coleridge,* ed. Kathleen Coburn (in progress). 6 double vols. New York, 1957–.

————. *Biographia Literaria,* ed. J. Shawcross. 2 vols. Oxford, 1962.

————. *Coleridge's Shakespearean Criticism,* ed. T. M. Raysor. 2 vols. London, 1960.

————. *Coleridge's Writings on Shakespeare,* ed. Terence Hawkes. New York, 1959. Introduction by Alfred Harbage.

Collier, John Payne. *The History of English Dramatic Poetry to the Time of Shakespeare: And Annals of the Stage to the Restoration.* 3 vols. London, 1831.

————. *Notes and Emendations to the Text of Shakespeare's Plays.* London, 1853.

Corson, Hiram. *An Introduction to the Study of Shakespeare.* Boston, 1889.

Criswell, R. W. *The New Shakspere and other travesties.* New York, 1882.

Cunningham, Peter. *Extracts from the Accounts of the Revels at Court, in the Reigns of Queen Elizabeth and King James.* London, 1842.

131

Dallas, E. S. *The Gay Science.* 2 vols. London, 1866.

————. *Poetics: An Essay on Poetry.* London, 1852.

Douce, Francis. *Illustrations of Shakespeare.* 2 vols. London, 1807.

Douglas, Lord Alfred. *The True History of Shakespeare's Sonnets.* London, 1933.

Dowden, Edward. "Beget and Begetter," *Athenaeum,* 3776 (March 24, 1900), 379.

————. "Elizabethan Psychology," *Atlantic Monthly* (September, 1907), 388–99.

————. *Introduction to Shakespeare.* New York, 1905.

————. *Letters of Edward Dowden and His Correspondents.* London, 1914.

————. *Poems.* London, 1914.

————. *Shakspere.* London, 1877.

————. *Shakspere: A Critical Study of His Mind and Art.* London, 1875; 3rd ed., New York, 1918.

————, ed. *The Sonnets of William Shakespeare.* London, 1889.

————. *Studies in Literature 1789–1877.* London, 1889.

————. *Transcripts and Studies.* London, 1896.

Drake, Nathan. *Shakspeare and His Times.* Paris, 1838.

Duncan, Joseph E. *The Revival of Metaphysical Poetry.* Minneapolis, 1959.

Dyce, Alexander. *A Glossary to the Works of William Shakespeare.* London, 1902.

Ebisch, Walther, and Levin L. Schücking. *A Shakespeare Bibliography.* Oxford, 1931.

The Economist 1843–1943. London, 1943.

Edwards, Thomas. *Canons of Criticism.* 6th ed. London, 1758. (The concluding remarks on Henry VIII (pp. 225–28) are generally referred to as "On the Metre of Henry VIII.")

Eglinton, John (pseud. for William K. Magee). *Irish Literary Portraits.* London, 1939.

Eliot, George. *Adam Bede.* London, 1859.

————. *The George Eliot Letters,* ed. Gordon S. Haight. 7 vols. New Haven, 1954–56.

————. *Middlemarch*, ed. Gordon S. Haight. Cambridge, Mass., 1956.

Eliot, T. S. *Shakespeare and the Stoicism of Seneca*. London, 1927.

Elze, Friedrich Karl. *Essays on Shakespeare*. London, 1874.

Empson, William. *Seven Types of Ambiguity*. London, 1956.

————. *Some Versions of Pastoral*. London, 1935.

Evans, Ifor Leslie. *The Language of Shakespeare's Plays*. London, 1952.

Fleay, Frederick Gard. *A Biographical Chronicle of the English Drama 1559–1642*. 2 vols. London, 1891.

————. *A Chronicle History of the Life and Work of William Shakespeare*. London, 1886.

————. *A Chronicle History of the London Stage, 1559–1642*. London, 1890.

————. *Egyptian Chronology: An Attempt to Conciliate the Ancient Schemes and to Educe a Rational System*. London, 1899.

————. "On the Motive of Shakspere's Sonnets," *Macmillan's Magazine* (May, 1875), 433–45.

————. *Shakespeare Manual*. London, 1876.

Fluchère, Henri. *Shakespeare*. London, 1953.

Friedman, William F., and Elizabeth S. *The Shakespearean Ciphers Examined*. Cambridge, 1957.

Fripp, Edgar I. *Shakespeare's Haunts Near Stratford*. London, 1929.

————. *Shakespeare, Man and Artist*. 2 vols. London, 1938.

Fuller, Thomas. *Worthies of England*, ed. John Freeman. London, 1952.

Furness, Helen Kate (Rogers). *A Concordance to Shakespeare's Poems*. Philadelphia, 1875.

Furness, Horace Howard. *The Letters of Horace Howard Furness*, ed. H. H. F. J. 2 vols. Boston, 1922.

Furnivall, Frederick James. "A Brief for the Defendant," *The Arena*, ed. B. O. Flower, VII (1892), 441–49.

————. *An English Miscellany to Dr. Furnivall*. Oxford, 1901.

————. *Mr. Swinburne's "Flat Burglary" on Shakspere*. London, 1879.

————. *The Succession of Shakspere's Works . . . : Being the Intro-duction to Professor Gervinus's 'Commentaries on Shakspere.'* London, 1874.

————. *Frederick James Furnivall: A Volume of Personal Record.* Oxford, 1911.

Furnivallos Furioso! and "The Newest Shakespeare Society": A Dram-attic Squib of the Period. In Three Fizzes, and Let Off for the Occasion, by the Ghost of Guido Fawkes! [Anonymous (A. C. Swinburne?). Attributed to John Jeremiah.] London, 1876.

Gardner, Helen. *The Business of Criticism.* Oxford, 1959.

Gervinus, George G. *Schriften zur Literatur,* ed. Gotthard Erler. Berlin, 1962.

————. *Shakespeare Commentaries,* trans. F. E. Bunnett. London, 1892.

Goethe, Johann Wolfgang von. *Wilhelm Meister's Apprenticeship.* Berlin, 1795; trans. Thomas Carlyle, New York, 1959.

Gollancz, Israel, ed. *A Book of Homage to Shakespeare.* Oxford, 1916.

Gottfried, Leon A. *Matthew Arnold and the Romantics.* Lincoln, Neb., 1963.

Greenberg, Robert A. "Walter Bagehot, Victorian Critic." Ph.D. dissertation. New York University, 1957.

Greg, Walter Wilson, ed. *Catalogue of the Books Presented by Edward Capell to the Library of Trinity College in Cambridge.* Cambridge, 1903.

————. *The Editorial Problem in Shakespeare.* 3d ed. Oxford, 1954.

————. *The Shakespeare First Folio.* Oxford, 1955.

Greg, William Rathbone. *The Creed of Christendom.* Toronto, 1878.

————. *Miscellaneous Essays.* Second Series. London, 1884.

Halliday, F. E. *A Shakespeare Companion 1550–1950.* New York, 1952.

————. *The Poetry of Shakespeare's Plays.* London, 1954.

————. *Shakespeare and His Critics.* London, 1958.

————. *Unfamiliar Shakespeare.* London, 1962.

Halliwell-Phillipps, J. O. *A Collection of Ancient Documents Respecting the Office of Master of the Revels.* London, 1870.

————. *Life of William Shakespeare.* London, 1848.

————. *Outlines of the Life of Shakespeare.* London, 1882.

————. *Which Shall It Be? New Lamps or Old? Shaxpere or Shakespeare?* Brighton, 1879.

Harris, Frank. *The Man Shakespeare and His Tragic Life Story.* New York, 1909.

————. *The Women of Shakespeare.* London, 1911.

Hazlitt, William. *The Complete Works of William Hazlitt,* ed. P. P. Howe. 21 vols. London, 1930–34.

Hegel, Friedrich. *Hegel on Tragedy,* eds. Anne and Henry Paolucci. New York, 1962.

Herford, C. H. *A Sketch of Recent Shakespearean Investigation.* London, 1923.

Hinman, Charlton. *The Printing and Proof-Reading of the First Folio of Shakespeare.* 2 vols. Oxford, 1963.

Hodges, C. Walter. *The Globe Restored.* New York, 1954.

Holloway, John. *The Victorian Sage.* London, 1953.

Hornstein, Lillian. "Analysis of Imagery: A Critique of Literary Method," *PMLA,* LVII (1942), 638–53.

Houghton, Walter E. *The Victorian Frame of Mind 1830–1870.* New Haven, 1957.

Hulme, Hilda M. *Explorations in Shakespeare's Language.* London, 1962.

Hyman, Stanley Edgar. *The Armed Vision.* New York, 1955.

Ingleby, Clement M. *A Complete View of the Shakspere Controversy Concerning the Genuineness of the Manuscript Matter Published by Collier.* London, 1861.

————. *Shakespeare, The Man and the Book.* 2 vols. London, 1877, 1881.

Irving, Laurence H. *Henry Irving.* New York, 1951.

Jaggard, William. *Shakespeare Bibliography.* Stratford-on-Avon, 1911.

Jahrbuch der deutschen Shakespeare-Gesellschaft. 1865–. Published principally in Weimar.

James, David G. *Matthew Arnold and the Decline of English Romanticism.* Oxford, 1961.

Jameson, Mrs. Anna B. *Shakespeare's Heroines; Characteristics of Women.* London, 1879.

Jeaffreson, John Cordy. *A Book of Recollections.* 2 vols. London, 1894.

Jeremiah, John. *Notes on Shakespeare.* London, 1876.

————. *Shakespearean Memorabilia.* London, 1877.

Johnson, Samuel. *Samuel Johnson on Shakespeare,* ed. W. K. Wimsatt, Jr. New York, 1960.

————. *Johnson's Chief Lives of the Poets,* ed. Matthew Arnold. London, 1879.

Katalog der Bibliothek der deutschen Shakespeare-Gesellschaft. Weimar, 1909.

Keats, John. *The Letters of John Keats, 1814–1821,* ed. Hyder Edward Rollins. 2 vols. Cambridge, Mass., 1958.

————. *The Poetical Works of John Keats,* ed. H. W. Garrod. 2d ed. Oxford, 1958.

Keller, Wolfgang. "Alois Brandl," *Shakespeare-Jahrbuch,* Band 77, 199–202. Weimar, 1941.

Kenny, Thomas. *The Life and Genius of Shakespeare.* London, 1864.

Kermode, Frank, ed. *The Tempest.* Arden Edition. Cambridge, Mass., 1958.

Kettle, Arnold. *An Introduction to the English Novel.* 2 vols. Rev. ed. London, 1959.

Knight, Charles. *Passages from the Life of Charles Knight.* New York, 1874.

————. *The Pictorial Edition of the Works of Shakspere.* 8 vols. London, 1843.

Knight, G. Wilson. *The Sovereign Flower.* London, 1958.

Knights, Lionel C. *Explorations: Essays in Criticism Mainly on the Literature of the Seventeenth Century.* New York, 1947.

————. *Some Shakespearean Themes.* London, 1959.

Langbaum, Robert W. *The Poetry of Experience.* New York, 1957.

Lascelles, Mary. *Shakespeare's Measure for Measure.* London, 1953.

Lawrence, William W. *Shakespeare's Problem Comedies.* New York, 1931.

Leavis, Frank R. *The Common Pursuit*. New York, 1952.

——. "A Retrospect," in *Scrutiny XX*, Cambridge, 1963.

——. *Two Cultures? The Significance of C. P. Snow*. London, 1962.

Lee, Sidney. *A Life of William Shakespeare*. New York, 1898.

——, ed. *Facsimile of the First Folio*. Oxford, 1902.

Losh, James. *The Diaries and Correspondence of James Losh*. 2 vols. London, 1962, 1963.

Luce, Morton. *Shakespeare*. Bristol, 1913.

Mabie, Hamilton Wright. *William Shakespeare*. New York, 1900.

MacCallum, M. W. *Shakespeare's Roman Plays and Their Background*. London, 1910.

MacKail, J. W. *The Approach to Shakespeare*. Oxford, 1930.

McLuhan, Marshall. *The Gutenberg Galaxy*. London, 1962.

Madden, D. H. *The Diary of Master William Silence*. London, 1907.

Maeterlinck, Maurice. "Macbeth," *L'Illustration Theatrale* No. 123. (Paris, 28 Aout, 1909).

——. *The Measure of the Hours*. New York, 1907.

Malone, Edmond. *An Account of the Incidents from Which the Title and Part of the Story of Shakespeare's Tempest Were Derived, and Its True Date Ascertained*. London, 1808.

Marder, Louis. *His Exits and His Entrances: The Story of Shakespeare's Reputation*. Philadelphia, 1963.

Maurer, Oscar. "Swinburne vs. Furnivall," *Texas University Studies in English*, 1952, pp. 86–96.

Meisel, Martin. *Shaw and the Nineteenth-Century Theatre*. Princeton, 1963.

Moulton, Richard G. *The Moral System of Shakespeare: A Popular Illustration of Fiction as the Experimental Side of Philosophy*. London, 1903.

——. *Shakespeare as a Dramatic Artist: A Popular Illustration of the Principles of Scientific Criticism*. London, 1885; London, 1906.

Moulton, W. Fiddian. *Richard Green Moulton: A Memoir*. Foreword by Sir Michael E. Sadler. New York, 1926.

Munby, A. N. L. *Phillipps Studies 1–5*. Cambridge, 1951–60.

Murry, John Middleton. *Keats and Shakespeare*. London, 1925; London, 1958.

Nelson, James G. *The Sublime Puritan*. Madison, Wisconsin, 1963.

New Shakspere Society, *Transactions*, 1874, 1875–76, 1877–79, 1880–86, 1887–92. London.

Newton, A. Edward. *The Amenities of Book Collecting*. Boston, 1918.

———. *The Greatest Book in the World*. Boston, 1925.

Ogden, C. K., and Richards, I. A. *The Meaning of Meaning*. London, 1930; New York, 1936.

Onions, C. T. *A Shakespeare Glossary*. London, 1911.

Palmer, John L. *Political and Comic Characters of Shakespeare*. London, 1961.

Patmore, Coventry. *Principle in Art*. London, 1889.

———. *Religio Poetae*. London, 1893.

Pollard, Alfred W. *Shakespeare Folios and Quartos: A Study in the Bibliography of Shakespeare's Plays, 1594–1685*. London, 1909.

———, *et al. Shakespeare's Hand in the Play of Sir Thomas More*. Cambridge, 1923.

Price, Hereward T. *Construction in Shakespeare*. University of Michi-
Pott, Mrs. Henry. *The Promus of Francis Bacon*. Boston, 1883.
gan Contribution in Modern Philology, No. 17. Ann Arbor, May, 1951.

Prince, T. R. *Shakespeariana*. London, 1889.

Proctor, Robert. *Bibliographical Essays*. London, 1905.

Ralli, Augustus. *A History of Shakespearian Criticism*. 2 vols. London, 1932.

Richards, I. A. *Coleridge on Imagination*. Bloomington, Indiana, 1960.

———. *Goodbye Earth*. New York, 1958.

———. *How to Read a Page*. New York, 1942; Boston, 1961.

———. *Meaning of Meaning*. London, 1930; New York, 1946 (see Ogden).

———. *Principles of Literary Criticism*. London, 1924.

————. *The Screens and Other Poems.* New York, 1960.

Ridler, Anne, ed. *Shakespeare Criticism 1919–1935.* London, 1936.

————. *Shakespeare Criticism 1935–1960.* London, 1963.

Rolfe, William J. *A Life of William Shakespeare.* Boston, 1904.

Rosenberg, Marvin. *The Masks of Othello.* Berkeley and Los Angeles, 1961.

Rowe, Nicholas, ed. *The Works of Mr. William Shakespear in Six Volumes.* London, 1709.

Rushton, William Lowes. *Shakespeare a Lawyer.* London, 1858.

————. *Shakespeare an Archer.* Liverpool, 1897.

Schelling, Felixe E. *The English Chronicle Play.* New York, 1902.

————. *Elizabethan Drama 1558–1642.* 2 vols. Boston, 1910.

Schmidt, Alexander. *Shakespeare-Lexicon.* 2 vols. Berlin, 1874–75.

Shakespeare, William. *The Plays and Poems of William Shakespeare in Ten Volumes.* Ed. Edmond Malone. London, 1790.

————. *The Plays and Poems of William Shakespeare. With a Life of the Poet and an Enlarged History of the Stage.* By the late E. Malone. Ed. J. Boswell. 21 vols. London, 1821.

————. The *Cambridge* edition, ed. W. G. Clark, J. Glover, and W. Aldis Wright. 9 vols. London, 1863–66.

————. The *Globe* edition, ed. W. G. Clark and W. A. Wright. London, 1864.

————. *A New Variorum Edition of Shakespeare,* ed. Horace Howard Furness. Philadelphia, 1871–.

————. *The Henry Irving Edition,* ed. Henry Irving and F. A. Marshall. 8 vols. London, 1887–90.

————. *New Arden Shakespeare.* London, in progress.

The Shakespeare Society, Publications of. London, 1841–53.

Shakespeariana conducted by the Shakespeare Society of New York. Philadelphia, 1883–93.

Shaw, Bernard. "Troilus and Cressida," B. M. Add. MSS. 50609.

Simpson, Richard. *An Introduction to the Philosophy of Shakespeare's Sonnets.* London, 1868.

————, ed. *The School of Shakspere.* 2 vols. London, 1878.

Singer, Samuel Weller. *The Text of Shakespeare Vindicated from the Interpolations and Corruptions Advocated by John Payne Collier Esq. in His Notes and Emendations.* London, 1853.

Sisson, C. J. *New Readings in Shakespeare.* 2 vols. Cambridge, 1956.

Smith, David Nichol, ed. *Eighteenth-Century Essays on Shakespeare.* 2nd ed. Oxford, 1963.

———. *Shakespeare Criticism: A Selection, 1623–1840.* Oxford, 1916.

Snow, C. P. *Science and Government.* Cambridge, Mass., 1961.

———. *The Two Cultures and a Second Look.* Cambridge, 1964.

Spalding, William. *A Letter on Shakespeare's Authorship of the Two Noble Kinsmen.* London, 1876.

Spedding, James. *The Letters and the Life of Francis Bacon.* 7 vols. London, 1861–74.

Spurgeon, Caroline F. E. *Keats's Shakespeare: A Descriptive Study.* Oxford, 1928.

———. *Shakespeare's Imagery and What It Tells Us.* Cambridge, 1935.

Stephen, Leslie. *Studies of a Biographer.* 4 vols. London, 1902.

Stewart, Dugald. *Philosophical Essays.* Edinburgh, 1810.

Stopes, Mrs. L. L. *Shakespeare's Environment.* London, 1914.

Strachey, Lytton, "Shakespeare's Final Period," *Independent Review,* III (Aug., 1904), 405–18. Reprinted in *Books and Characters.* London, 1922.

Sugden, Edward H. *A Topographical Dictionary to the Works of Shakespeare and His Fellow Dramatists.* Manchester, 1925.

Swinburne, Algernon Charles. *The Complete Works of Algernon Charles Swinburne,* eds., Sir Edmund Gosse, C. B., and Thomas James Wise. 20 vols. London, 1925–27.

———. *Essays and Studies.* London, 1875.

———. "John Webster," *The Nineteenth Century and After* (1886), 861–81.

———. *A Study of Shakespeare.* London, 1880.

———. *The Swinburne Letters,* ed. Cecil Lang. 6 vols. New Haven, 1959–62.

ten Brink, Bernhard. *Five Lectures on Shakespeare.* London, 1895.

Terry, Ellen. *Four Lectures on Shakespeare.* London, 1932.

Thomson, James (B. V.). *Satires and Profanities.* London, 1884.

Tilley, M. P. *A Dictionary of the Proverbs in England in the Sixteenth and Seventeenth Centuries.* Ann Arbor, 1950.

Tillyard, E. M. W. *Shakespeare's Problem Plays.* Toronto, 1949.

Times Literary Supplement. "Scholars at Work (1837–1937)," May 1, 1937, pp. 334–35.

————. "Shakespeare's Day," April 23, 1964, pp. 331–64.

Tobacco: Its History Illustrated by the Books, Manuscripts, and Engravings in the Library of George Arents, Jr. 5 vols. New York, Rosenbach Company, 1937–52. Introduction by Jerome Brooks.

"The Tribunal of Literary Criticism, Bacon vs. Shakespeare," *The Arena,* ed. B. O. Flower, VI–VIII (Boston, 1892–93).

Trilling, Lionel. *Matthew Arnold.* New York, 1955.

Turnell, Martin. *The Art of French Fiction.* New York, 1959.

Walker, William Sidney. *A Critical Examination of the Text of Shakespeare.* 3 vols. London, 1860.

Ward, Adolphus William. *A History of English Dramatic Literature to the Death of Queen Anne.* 3 vols. 2d rev. ed. London, 1899.

Ward, Aileen. *John Keats.* New York, 1963.

Ward, Thomas Humphrey, ed. *The English Poets.* 5 vols. (Selections with critical introductions by various writers and a general introduction by Matthew Arnold.) New York, 1880–1918.

Warren, Alba H. *English Poetic Theory 1825–1865.* Princeton, 1950.

Wendell, Barrett. *William Shakspere.* New York, 1894.

West, Rebecca. *The Court and the Castle.* New Haven, 1957.

White, Beatrice. "Frederick James Furnivall," *Essays and Studies.* (London, 1952), 64–76.

Whiter, Walter. *A Specimen of a Commentary on Shakspeare Containing: I. Notes on As You Like It. II. An Attempt to Explain and Illustrate Various Passages, on a New Principle of Criticism Derived from Mr. Locke's Doctrine of the Association of Ideas.* London, 1794.

Wilde, Oscar. *The Portrait of Mr. W. H.* London, 1899.

Willey, Basil. *Nineteenth Century Studies.* New York, 1950.

――――. *More Nineteenth Century Studies.* New York, 1956.

Wilson, Frank Perry. *Marlowe and the Early Shakespeare.* Oxford, 1953.

Wilson, John Dover, ed. *Hamlet.* Cambridge, 1934.

――――. *The Manuscript of Shakespeare's Hamlet and the Problems of Its Transmission.* 2 vols. Cambridge, 1934. Reprinted with additions, Cambridge, 1963.

――――. *What Happens in Hamlet.* 3d ed. Cambridge, 1951.

Winstanley, D. A. "Halliwell-Phillipps and Trinity College Library," *Library*, 5th Ser., II, no. 4 (March, 1948), 250–82.

Wise, Thomas J. *Letters of Thomas J. Wise to John Henry Wrenn,* ed. Fannie E. Ratchford. New York, 1944.

Wordsworth, Charles. *On Shakespeare's Knowledge and Use of the Bible.* London, 1864.

Wordsworth, William. *The Complete Poetical Works of Wordsworth.* Cambridge, Mass., 1932.

Wright, Joseph. *The English Dialect Dictionary.* 6 vols. London, 1898–1905.

Young, G. M. "The Case for Walter Bagehot," *Spectator* (July 2, 1937), pp. 9–10.

――――. "The Greatest Victorian," *Spectator* (June 18, 1937), 1137–38. See also Rebuttal, "The Greatest Victorian" (June 25, 1937), 1190.

――――. *Victorian England.* New York, 1954.

Zabel, Morton D. *The Romantic Idealism of Art 1800–1848.* Chicago, 1938.

Inðex

The text for *Shakespeare and the Victorians* has been set on the Linotype in 11½-point Caslon, a faithful rendering of one of the original type faces designed by William Caslon. The paper on which the book is printed bears the watermark of the University of Oklahoma Press and has an effective life of at least three hundred years.